PRINCIPLES OF EDUCATION

MAVEN BOOKS

PRINCIPLES OF EDUCATION

MALCOLM MACVICAR, PH.D., L.L.D

Former Principal State Normal and Training School, Potsdam, N.Y. First Chancellor of McMaster University, Toronto, Ont.

MAVEN BOOKS

Chennai　　　　Trichy　　　　New Delhi

MAVEN BOOKS

This edition has been published in india by arrangement with Carson Books, UK

ISBN 978-93-90877-51-5   Maven Books

All rights reserved   No. 44, Nallathambi Street,
Triplicane, Chennai 600 005

MJP 1056   © Publishers, 2021

Publisher :   C. Janarthanan

Publisher's Note

The legacy of a country is in its varied cultural heritage, historical literature, developments in the field of economy and science. The top nations in the world are competing in the field of science, economy and literature. This vast legacy has to be conserved and documented so that it can be bestowed to the future generation. The knowledge of this legacy is slowly getting perished in the present generation due to lack of documentation.

Keeping this in mind, the concern with retrospective acquiring of rare books has been accented recently by the burgeoning reprint industry. Maven Books is gratified to retrieve the rare collections with a view to bring back those books that were landmarks in their time.

In this effort, a series of rare books would be republished under the banner, "Maven Books". The books in the reprint series have been carefully selected for their contemporary usefulness as well as their historical importance within the intellectual. We reconstruct the book with slight enhancements made for better presentation, without affecting the contents of the original edition.

Most of the works selected for republishing covers a huge range of subjects, from history to anthropology. We believe this reprint edition will be a service to the numerous researchers and practitioners active in this fascinating field. We allow readers to experience the wonder of peering into a scholarly work of the highest order and seminal significance.

MAVEN BOOKS

INTRODUCTORY NOTE.

In preparing every part of the outline contained in this small volume the aim has been, not to give an exhaustive analysis or discussion of the subjects presented, but to furnish material that will provoke investigation and thought and that will render, at the same time, practical help to teachers and others interested in the education of the young. The outline is given in the form of propositions, followed by brief notes, which serve to explain or call attention to the truths which the propositions explicitly state or imply. These notes, being necessarily brief, present only in a partial way the views of their author. No attempt is made to discuss fundamental truths regarding matter and mind, life and development, on which both the propositions and notes are based. It is hoped, however, that the propositions and notes are sufficiently full and explicit to be clearly understood and to serve the practical purposes for which they are intended. With this hope they are submitted for the consideration and assistance of co-workers in educational effort.

CONTENTS.

PRINCIPLES OF EDUCATION.

GENERAL PRINCIPLES.

Under this head will be noted those principles of education which underlie every well directed effort for the symmetrical development of a human being, and also the classification and nature of true educational products.

1. *An impartial and careful examination of the whole phenomena of life reveals clearly three great classes, viz.: Vegetal Life, Animal Life, and Mind Life.*

(*a*). The exact line which separates these three classes of life may be difficult to determine ; yet, notwithstanding this, the fact of the existence of the three classes cannot, upon any sound principles of classification, be rejected. It is, perhaps, well to note here that there exists no more difficulty in determining the line of separation between Mind Life and Animal Life, than between Animal Life and Vegetal Life.

(*b*). Each one of these three classes of life has its own peculiar laws of growth or development, and hence each class is, in a certain sense, alike susceptible of education. The fundamental problem, therefore, of education is the discovery and application of these laws; hence the careful study of biology and psychology is of first importance to the true educator.

2. *Each individual life originates in a parent life, and derives from that parent life its inherent constitution.*

(*a*). This proposition is now generally conceded by scientific authorities. Belief in spontaneous generation is a thing of the past.

(*b*). What life is in itself is still a disputed question. Two views commonly prevail upon the subject. It is maintained on the one hand that life is the product of physical forces, and on the other that it is an independent and distinct entity or endowment. The latter is the view adopted in these notes.

(*c*). Adopting the latter view, it is maintained that the life is the organizing power which selects and disposes of the material, physical and otherwise, which compose and perpetuate each organ of the body and faculty of the mind. It is maintained, also, that the life alone determines the nature and extent of the possibilities inherent in both body and mind.

(*d*). The parent life bestows upon its offspring its own type of life and organism. This includes what may be called the natural or original type, and also such changes in life and organism as may have been acquired by the parent life. The acquired power or dexterity, for example, of some organ or faculty as well as the original type, may be transmitted from parent to offspring.

3. The process of education, in a broad sense, may be defined as that by which external conditions or appliances are made, by the action of an agent, the means of unfolding or developing symmetrically all the legitimate possibilities of a single life.

(*a*). The word education is commonly used in two senses. It is used, as in this definition, to denote a process, but it is also used to denote the result or product of the process. As a process, a true and complete education means the course of training, instruction and discipline through which a human being must pass to acquire the full and legitimate exercise of all the organs of the body, the full and legitimate exercise of all the powers of the mind, and so much systematized knowledge as will fit him to use, in an intelligent and efficient manner, the organs of his body and powers of his mind, in performing physical, intellectual, moral and spiritual work. As a result or product, a true education means a symmetrically developed body and mind, possessed of power, right habits, pure and elevated tastes, and systematized knowledge.

(*b*). A true and complete education, in accordance with this definition, is a growth, a development, an evolution (using the term evolution in a restricted sense), of all the possibilities which God has implanted in our nature; it is the unifying of these possibilities subordinating them all to the control of the will; it is, in short, the crystallization of all these possibilities into a pure and noble character. This result is the product of the joint action of inherent natural powers, and environments supplied by parents, teachers and other agencies.

(*c*). The process of education, in whatever way it may be carried on, involves three factors : namely, the teacher, the pupil, and the instrumentalities by which the teacher affects the pupil, or by which a vitalizing union is constituted between the pupil and what is external to him. The word teacher, in this connection, is used to include any agent who directs and controls the instrumentalities by which the pupil is affected, hence the parents and the pupils themselves are included. When the pupils become their own agents in carrying on the work, the process is called self-education.

4. *Man, in all educational processes, must be regarded as an organized unit, composed of body and mind, united in such a manner that no one element of this complex whole can be developed, or in any way affected, without in some degree affecting the entire being.*

(*a*). The popular classification of education into physical, intellectual, moral and spiritual, is very misleading. It attracts attention from the absolute unity of our being. It causes many to suppose that the process of education is actually separable into four departments, each of which can be carried on absolutely independent of all the others. Those falling into this error find it difficult to understand why the

Bible, which is the peculiar basis of spiritual education, should be a necessary element of physical and intellectual education.

(*b*). Conflicting philosophical views prevail as to the real existence of the two substances—matter and mind. The materialist, on the one hand, maintains that matter is the only existing substance, and that the phenomena of thought, feeling and will are evolved from this substance. The idealist, on the other hand, maintains that mind is the only substance that has any real existence, and that all phenomena attributed to matter are necessarily phenomena evolved from mind. These are the two extreme views. A third view maintains the existence of the two substances, matter and mind, each being the source or origin of phenomena, which cannot upon any principles of sound reasoning, be derived from the other. This view holds that existing phenomena can be accounted for only by accepting the real and equally original and independent existence of matter and mind, both substances being mysteriously united in the constitution, and hence in the production of the phenomena of the complex unit called man. This is not the place to discuss or defend the merits of any one of these views. It is perhaps sufficient to say that the last-stated is the view adopted in these notes.

(*c*). The unity of the body and mind, and the power of what may be called the law of reflex action in the development of both, is established beyond doubt by the most careful scientific observation and experiment. It is an obvious fact, even to common observers, that in the most minute details the body affects the mind, and the mind the body. Diseases of the body, for example, are not unfrequently the direct products of the reflex action of the mind.

(*d*). The law of reflex action extends much further than is usually supposed. It takes in the entire man. Not only does the body affect the mind, and the mind the body, in a general sense, but each organ of the body has a reflex influence over every other organ, and each faculty of the mind over every other faculty. There is a perfect interdependence running through the entire being. It is literally true, whether we refer to body or mind or to the union of both, that "if one member suffers all the members suffer with it, or if one member be honored all the members rejoice with it." In view, then, of the power and ever-operative nature of the law of *reflex action*, it is evident that the physical and intellectual natures cannot be symmetrically developed independent of a corresponding and parallel development of the moral and spiritual natures.

(*e*). It may be here observed, that this proposition deserves from every teacher careful consideration, as it states one of the most fundamental conditions upon which a true philosophy of education must rest. Unless the real unity of man's being and the real reciprocal dependence of all the elements composing that unity are fully recognized, all educational processes and efforts, however well devised and well directed, must ever fail of the best results, must ever fail of producing a symmetrical manhood.

5. Man as an organized unit is possessed of two distinct, and yet related and mutually dependent, classes of possibilities: namely, physical possibilities and mental possibilities.

(*a*). The word *possibilities* is used in these notes to mean the qualities, properties, powers, or faculties inherent in an individual life and its organism, through which such life and organism are capable of growth or development, and of sustaining definite and operative relations to the world of mind and matter. The word *organism* is also used to refer to the mind as well as to the body. Each is equally organized. They differ not in the fact that the body is organized and the mind not, but in the nature of the substance of which each is composed.

(*b*). The physical and mental organisms together constitute the unit man. Each organism, however, has possibilities which are exercised independent the one of the other. For example, there are various processes going on constantly in the body, such as the action of the heart, which are, in a certain sense, entirely independent of any action of the mind. There are, in like manner, in the higher regions of mental activity processes carried on which are equally independent of the body.

(*c*). While it is true that the physical and mental organisms each possess independent possibilities, it is also equally true that these possibilities cannot always be exercised independently. For example, the mind can have no consciousness of an external world, except through the activity of the organs of sense. But, still more, this dependence is of such a nature that there can be no healthy exercise even of the possibilities of the body or of the mind that are independent of each other, except as the possibilities whose exercise depends one on the other, and which bind the two organisms together as parts of one whole, are in full and healthy exercise.

6. *A true system of education must provide, at one and the same time, the conditions and appliances necessary for the separate and mutual development of the organs of the body, and of all the faculties of the mind.*

(*a*). The truth of this proposition follows necessarily from the two preceding propositions.

(*b*). Not only does the growth or development of the body and of the mind run parallel with each other in point of time, but the healthy development of the one is dependent upon the healthy development of the other. Neither can be neglected for a single day without doing injury to the other. Healthy physical growth, for example, is impossible where a certain minimum of mental activity is not maintained. The converse of this is equally true; hence the truth of the proposition.

(*c*). The principle stated in this proposition refers not only to the general relations of body and mind, but also to the special relations of the organs of the one and the faculties of the other. The principle assumes, for example, that the healthy development of the intellectual elements of a man's nature is inseparably connected with and dependent upon the healthy development of both the moral and spiritual elements. In this, the principle correctly assumes that these three, apparently distinct elements of man's nature are necessarily only three phases of the one indivisible unit called mind, and, hence, that the conditions and appliances used in conducting the educational process should, in their very nature, be such as will at the same time minister to the healthy development of each of these three elements.

EDUCATIONAL PRODUCTS.

7. *A careful examination and analysis of true educational products will, it is believed, justify classifying them under the following general heads :*

(*a*). Physical and mental power.
(*b*). Right habits.
(*c*). Pure and elevated tastes.
(*d*). Systematized knowledge.
(*e*). A reliable and symmetrical character.

In reference to each of these classes of educational products, the following propositions should be carefully noticed :

PHYSICAL AND MENTAL POWER.

8. *Power as an educational product is of two kinds: namely, Receptivity and Energy.*

(*a*). Receptivity is that form of power which enables man to receive impressions of all sorts, to endure, to bear, to suffer, to be influenced, to be trained to certain courses of feeling, thought and action.

(*b*). Energy, on the other hand, is that form of power which makes man a cause, which enables him to produce effects, to bring things to pass, to think, to act, to perform physical and mental work.

(*c*). Power as a receptivity, and also as an energy, is coextensive with man's entire being. Each organ of the body and faculty of the mind is endowed with power in each of these respects. This power is transmitted in its germinal form from parent to offspring, and is susceptible either of improvement or degeneracy, under conditions that will hereafter be noted.

(*d*). Power as a receptivity is the only channel through which education in any of its phases is made possible. Indeed, the degree of receptivity, in each case, determines the degree or extent to which the education of the individual can be carried. For example, it is impossible to educate a person possessed of low receptive power for slight variations of sound, so as to become a critical judge of artistic music.

(*e*). The degree to which power as an energy is possessed determines the effectiveness of each man in the conduct of whatever may be his life work. This is true, whether the man be viewed from the standpoint of physical or mental effort.

9. *Physical power is manifested through the two classes of organs of which the body is essentially composed: namely, the apparatus of organic life and the apparatus of animal life.*

(*a*). The function of the apparatus of organic life is to construct and to keep in working order every organ of the body; that of the apparatus of animal life is to place the mind in conscious and mechanical relations to the body itself and to the external world. The apparatus of animal life is composed—1st, of the cerebro-spinal nervous system, which includes the brain, spinal cord, and the nerves connected directly with these centres known as the sensory and motor nerves; 2d, the skeleton, which includes the bones, cartilages, and ligaments; and 3d, the muscles. These parts are united together in such a manner as to form two classes of devices, known as the sensory organs and the motor or mechanical organs.

(*b*). The body as a whole may be regarded as a complex machine, in which are located, at certain points, special devices or machines, composed of a combination of sensory nerves, motor nerves, bones and muscles, joined together and fitted to perform a special work. The feet, the hands, and the neck are illustrations of these devices. The hand, for example, is so constructed that it is capable of forming an almost endless variety of mechanical connections with external objects, and hence capable of performing a great variety of work.

(*c*). The structure of the sensory organs should be carefully noted. Each is not a simple device composed exclusively of a group of special sensory nerves. For example, the eyeball and the motor nerves and muscles by which it is moved form each a part of the organ of sight. The position in the body, and the reason why each organ is so placed, should also be noted. The fact that the eye, the ear, the nose, and the tongue are located in the head, and the touch spread over the entire body, is not a matter of chance.

(*d*). Each of the sensory organs, from its peculiar structure and position, is fitted to place the mind in conscious relation to only one class of phenomena in the external world. The eye connects the mind consciously with the phenomena of *color*, the touch with the phenomena of *resistance*, the ear with the phenomena of *sound*, the nose with the phenomena of *smell*, and the tongue with the phenomena of *taste*. These simple classes of phenomena, and their necessary consequences and combinations, constitute all that can be known through the senses of the objective or material world.

(*e*). No one of the five senses can place the mind in conscious relation to the phenomena which belong to another sense. The cases commonly known as a substitution of one sense for another are only apparent, not real. For example, it is supposed that a blind person can determine color by touch. In this case, where the person has been born blind, there never can be any consciousness of color. His apparent discrimination of colored objects is simply the result of his knowledge of the degree and nature of resistance substances give to the touch which are called blue, red, and so on. Hence he can pick out the objects that are blue or red, and speak of them as such as freely as a person who is actually conscious of the color. Another case, perhaps more to the point, is commonly cited, namely, determining extension by sight and touch. Here it is true that extension in a certain sense is given through each sense, but it must be noticed that the consciousness of extension given by the factor color through the sight is always sharply distinguished from the consciousness of the same extension given through the sense of touch.

(*f*). Our consciousness of objects in the external world is produced by the actual contact of these objects with the sensory nerves; hence all of the senses operate precisely in the same manner as touch. That which produces consciousness through the eye, the nose and the tongue, is as really in actual contact with the nerve in each case as that which produces it through the touch. For example, the consciousness of color and of extension, at least in two dimensions, is caused by the actual contact of light with the optic nerve.

(*g*). The motor organs are all subject to the direction and control of the mind, and have the power of forming habits. Hence they can be educated or trained so as to perform the work for which they are intended in an easy and efficient manner. This training should commence with the infant and continue through childhood and youth. It should receive the constant attention of both parents and teachers, as the strength and efficiency of the future man largely depend upon his ability to use effectively the mechanical organs.

(*h*). The power and efficiency of the sensory and mechanical organs depend upon the formation of right habits of work, and these habits can be formed only by persistently training each organ in doing its own special work. Right habits of work are the products of time and persistent practice. Yet much can be done to help the child in forming habits by a proper regard to the simple demands of his nature. Those demands suggest that, in order to form good habits of work, his course of training should be arranged so that none of the following conditions are violated:

(1). The special exercises for each organ should comprehend the entire range of work for which the organ is intended.

(2). The organs should be exercised in such combinations with each other as will occur in using them in actual life.

(3). The activity of the organs called into exercise should not produce present or future pain or suffering.

(4). The activity of the organs at every stage of the work should be sustained by a present and prospective purpose.

(5). Present results should always be arranged so that they require continued attention and repetition, in order that their full value may be realized.

10. *Mind as the source of power is constituted so as to sustain conscious and unconscious relations to entities and phenomena pertaining to space and its contents, to time and its contents, and to mind or spirit and its contents.*

(*a*). The mind is in no sense composed of parts which perform separate and distinct offices. It acts as an *indivisible unit* when it perceives, recalls what is past, wills, etc. While this is true, it is equally true that the mental energy exercised in perceiving and in willing, for example, can be clearly distinguished from each other, hence the various conscious manifestations of mental energy can be classified. This gives rise to the distinctions called *faculties*. A faculty, therefore, means the mind putting forth, as a *unit*, an energy which can be clearly distinguished from other manifestations of mental energy.

(*b*). The exercise of mental energy may be classified under eight heads, as follows: The energy exercised,

(1). In the act of perceiving or being conscious of what is now and here present to the mind;

(2). In the act of conserving or retaining out of consciousness knowledge or past experiences.

(3) In the act of reproducing or bringing back into consciousness past experiences.

(4). In the act of representing or holding up

before the mind all of which it has been or is conscious ;

(5). In the act of comparing or recognizing the
differences and agreements between two or more
objects of consciousness.

(6). In the act of desiring or choosing or prefer-
ring the presence of one kind of mental activity or
passivity to another ;

(7). In the act of willing or originating, continuing or changing any one or more of the activities of
the mind ;

(8). In the act of deciding *when, where, how* and
for what purpose the active or receptive power of the
mind *ought* to be exercised.

(*c*). Mental power as a *receptivity* is not, as in the
case of *energy*, susceptible of definite classification.
Its exercise is especially manifest in the phenomena
of pleasure and pain, habits, etc.

11. *Acquired power, either as a receptivity or as an
energy, is, in the first place, the product of a healthy
growth of the physical and mental organism.*

(*a*). A healthy growth is largely the product of a
proper supply of suitable food.   Body and mind are
alike dependent for their growth upon this condition.
The food of the former is *matter*, of the latter *truth*.
The food of each, in order that it may promote a
healthy growth of the organism, must be subjected
to the same process, namely, digestion and assimilation.   A healthy mental growth is just as dependent

upon the digestion and assimilation of *truth* as a healthy physical growth is dependent upon the digestion and assimilation of matter.

(*b*). Suitable food means such a combination and variety of physical and mental food, supplied at one and the same time, as contains all the elements that are necessary not only to develop bone and muscle and nerve, but also the more subtle organism of the mind. Only such food can minister properly to the healthy growth of both body and mind.

(*c*). It should be further carefully noted, that food, possessing the elements necessary to develop one phase of the organism, may be entirely lacking in the elements necessary to develop other phases. For example, food which is only fitted to produce muscular tissue, is lacking in some of the elements necessary to produce bone. In like manner such truth, or mental aliment, as is fitted to nourish only the intellectual phase of the mental organism, is lacking in what is necessary to supply nourishment to the moral and spiritual phases of this organism. Hence an educational process which supplies only, or even chiefly, an intellectual aliment must fail in developing moral and spiritual power.

12. *Power both as a receptivity and an energy is, in the second place, the product of the right or mutually dependent use of all the organs of the body and faculties of the mind.*

(*a*). Activity is one of the necessary laws of all

healthy growth or development. The activity of both the organs of the body and faculties of the mind is of two kinds, namely, that which originates entirely within these organs and faculties, and that which originates in an operative connection formed between them and what is outside of themselves. This latter is what is generally known as *work*. The continued and healthy existence of the former activity is dependent upon the latter. Any organ of the body or faculty of the mind, which becomes absolutely inactive in the latter sense, must also cease very soon to be active in the former.

(*b*). Body and mind are constructed so that the organs of the one and the faculties of the other are designed for work, or, in other words, are designed to accomplish certain definite ends or purposes outside of themselves. For example, the hand connects the body mechanically with the outside world, the eye sensitively or receptively, and the will causatively. In accomplishing the ends or purposes outside of themselves, it should be noted that the organs of the body and faculties of the mind are complementary to each other, and hence that the activity of the one is dependent upon the activity of the other.

(*c*). Power both as a receptivity and an energy is evolved or developed in the act of performing work as defined in (*a*) and (*b*). This fact is verified by universal experience. It is a matter of common observation, that use or work develops additional *energies* in the arm of the blacksmith, in the reasoning faculties of the mathematician and in the will of the man whose duty it is to control the action of others. It is equally a matter of common observation that use **or** work develops additional receptivity or sensitiveness in the eye of the artist, in the ear of the musician, in the imagination of the poet, in the perception of the thinker, in the conscience of the man of moral efforts, and in the spirit of the man who walks with God.

(*d*). It must be further observed that the evolution or development of power, in its fullest and best sense, requires the natural and unconstrained use of all the possibilities of the entire man. It requires such a use or work as will call into full systematic and harmonious exercise each organ of the body and faculty of the mind. This requires the continuous and regular adjustment of work and appliances to the actual condition of both organs and faculties as they progress from one stage of development to another.

13. *A careful analysis of the entire phenomena of power as an educational product will justify the following classification :*

<table>
<tr><td rowspan="2">Power.</td><td>I. Receptivity.</td><td rowspan="2">Each,</td><td>1. Physical.</td></tr>
<tr><td>II. Energy.</td><td>2. Intellectual.
3. Moral.
4. Spiritual.</td></tr>
</table>

(*a*). Physical, intellectual and moral power have, each of them, a germinal existence in the constitution of every human being, and are susceptible of development, as set forth in Arts. 11 and 12. Spiritual power begins also in a germ implanted in the constitution. Different views prevail, however, as to the nature and origin of this germinal power.   Reference will be made to this in the notes on the study of the English Bible. Here it must simply be observed that development results from spiritual aliment and spiritual activity.

(*b*). These four classes of phenomena, while necessarily blended together as the one manifestation of the complex unit man, are, nevertheless, separated one from the other by marked characteristics.   These characteristics are unmistakable, although, as in the case of vegetal and animal life, it may be difficult, if not impossible, to draw a sharp line of separation indicating definitely the boundary of each.   This is particularly true of intellectual, moral and spiritual power.   The following indicates in a general way the sphere in which each class of power manifests itself.

(*c*). Physical power manifests itself in feats of strength and agility, in graceful actions, in the artistic exercise of special organs of the body—as the hand—in handling tools of all sorts, in performing, by the use of tools, all kinds of work, in connecting through the organs of sense the mind with the external world, etc.

(*d*). Intellectual power manifests itself in thought, in searching into the nature of things, in discovering the origin and causes of all phenomena, in the acquisition and application of knowledge, in conducting courses of intricate and logical reasoning, etc.

(*e*). Moral power manifests itself in recognizing and enforcing the rights and obligations of self and of all men, in sympathetic and self-sacrificing efforts for the relief of all kinds of distress and suffering, and for the highest good of all men, in clear and well-defined perceptions of right and wrong, in exercising that kind of courage that dares to do right under all conditions and circumstances, etc.

(*f*). Spiritual power manifests itself in lifting up all that pertains to physical, intellectual and moral power into a life of consecration to God, a life of faith and works modeled after the life of Christ, etc.

RIGHT HABITS.

14. *Habits are induced states of the body or of the mind through which the power residing in each is effectively used in performing work or in accomplishing given ends without the conscious exercise of the intelligence and will.*

(*a*). It should be carefully noted that *taste* is very generally mistaken for *habits.* For example, we speak of a man forming the habit of using tobacco, drinking intoxicating liquors, and of reading trashy and immoral books. In such cases as this, what is formed is not a habit at all, but a strong and vitiated taste. Habit, as the definition indicates, is an induced state of the body or mind which fits a person for the exercise of the energy or power he possesses in performing some given work. Taste, on the other hand, attracts its possessor to some subjective enjoyment, or guides him in the execution of his ideals.

(*b*). In restricting the word habit to acquired or induced states of the body or mind, it is not intended to reject the fact, now so well established, that certain aptitudes of both body and mind are inherited. The cunning of the hand, the eye and the ear, as well as the power for certain subtle mental work, passes from the parent to the child. This is true, and such inherited aptitudes must be treated as a part of the child's original capital; but the educator is, however, specially interested in what can be added to this by acquisition.

(*c*). The body and mind are endowed with power. (Art. 8.)   Habit alone is the medium through which this power can be effectively utilized in performing work.   The truth of this statement may be readily shown by reference to any sort of mechanical skill. Take, for example, the hand; it is endowed naturally with the power of producing almost an infinite variety of motions. It is also subject, in a certain sense, to the direction of the mind.   Does this fit it to handle successfully tools of any sort?   All will answer emphatically, no.   Practice is needed in order to do this.   But what is meant by this practice?   Simply this, that a persistent and continuous repetition, through an effort of the intelligence and will, of the motions of the hand, necessary to do a given kind of work by the use of certain tools, induces a state of the organism concerned in producing these motions which we call habit. Just here it is very important, in order to locate rightly the teacher's work, that we note with some care the nature and use of these induced states or habits.

(*d*). In the above example the motions of the hand in using the tools are at first produced, very imperfectly and slowly, by the exercise of a strong effort of the intelligence and will. By persisting, however, in the practice, dexterity is gradually acquired, and the necessary effort of the intelligence and will gradually diminishes, until finally the work is performed with rapidity and case, and with almost no conscious effort. The formation of all habits, whether of body or mind, follows substantially the law here illustrated. It will therefore be observed that as rapidly as habits are perfectly formed, conserved physical and mental power can be applied almost, if not altogether, unconsciously, in the performance of work. In this case, the exercise of the intelligence and will ceases to be necessary to direct and control the muscular and nerve energy or mental energy by which the work is performed. When this point is reached, workmanship of a high order becomes possible. But why is this? The answer is plain. The mental energy, that was before required to handle and direct the tools, is now used in studying and perfecting the ideal as the work progresses; hence the improved results. Universal experience verifies this position. A first-class mechanic is, in every instance, a man who has converted the use of each tool that he handles into a perfect habit, and hence who is able, while doing a piece of work, to give his whole attention to shaping everything with reference to the finish and perfection of the work itself.

(*e*). What has just been stated as true of mechanical effort holds equally true of all departments of art. Finger and foot movements, for example, in piano and organ music, must become habits or unconscious acts before the player can produce any effects of a high order. To produce such effects, the intelligence and will must be perfectly free and directed to the ideal which the artist seeks to make real in his own mind and in the mind of his hearers. Painters, sculptors, orators and artists of every sort are equally as dependent as the musician upon the adaptation and perfection of the habits formed. They can never produce a high order of results, until, by the formation of habits, the power of the intelligence and will is left entirely free to be used in studying and shaping effects, rather than in directing and guiding purely mechanical movements.

(*f*). It should further be noted that habits are no more necessary as conditions of efficient work where the body plays so important a part than they are where mind alone is concerned. A single example will illustrate this. The power of continued attention is a *habit* or induced state of the mind. In the case of very young children this power scarcely exists. This is also true to a large extent of persons of mature years. In the first attempt at real study it requires a struggle, a strong effort of the will, to hold the mind continuously upon one point. This fact is clear in every person's experience. But there is another fact equally clear, namely, that the persistent and continuous effort of the will in holding the attention induces a state of mind in which the exercise of this will-power becomes gradually less and less necessary. Indeed, as in the case of the use of tools, so in this, the point may be reached where the conscious exercise of the will is only necessary to initiate the act of attention. This is exactly the condition of persons who, when their attention is turned to a subject, become entirely unconscious of their surroundings, and of everything but the matter under consideration.

(*g*). In view of what has just been stated, a man properly fitted to be an efficient worker, either with his body or mind, is in a very real sense, a " bundle of habits." This fact is not sufficiently recognized. The acquisition of knowledge, and not habits, is the chief if not the only end of the educational efforts of our schools and colleges. This is certainly a great mistake. In this course the fact is overlooked that certain kinds of knowledge are of little or no value, unless accompanied by corresponding habits. As an example of this may be named a knowledge of grammar, composition or rhetoric. A pupil may acquire a very complete knowledge of all the facts and principles of grammar and rhetoric, and yet be utterly unable to speak or write correctly. To become able to speak or write correctly is not the product of knowledge, but of habit. Hence it comes to pass, not unfrequently, that persons, entirely ignorant of grammar, as taught in our schools, speak and write the English language more correctly than many who have spent years in acquiring an exhaustive technical knowledge of the subject.

(*h*). It should here be carefully noted that in the entire range of subjects which compose an elementary education, the chief thing to be acquired is not knowledge, but habits. This must be evident to every educator who has given the subject any consideration. In all elementary work the acquisition of the art of doing is the *important thing*, and should receive *first* attention. A perfect knowledge, for example, of all the rules that have ever been made regarding reading will never make a good reader. The power to read with expression means the acquisition of an art; it means the training of organs, and hence the formation of habits. But what is true of reading is equally true of spelling, of writing, of arithmetic, of grammar, and of composition. In each of these subjects, the art or habit of doing certain things in a certain way is the chief object to be accomplished by both teacher and pupil.

(*i*). What is true in regard to the acquisition of habits in an elementary education is equally true of higher education. It should be observed, however, that after passing from the elementary to the more advanced stages of work, the habits acquired have reference not so much to the physical as to the intellectual, moral and spiritual factors of the nature. When habits of the right sort are not formed, with reference to each of these factors, the education is very imperfect; it means but very little. A wide range of knowledge may be acquired, but this will serve scarcely any purpose in real life. A large share of it must, in the very nature of things, disappear as soon as the school or college is left. What will be of real service in the life work is the man that the training afforded has produced. But the man does not mean knowledge, however valuable this may be; it means the power acquired and the habits and tastes formed by which this power can be utilized. It is the acquisition of these alone that will make the man felt in his contact with his fellows, and that will give him success in whatever calling in life he may engage.

(*j*). From the foregoing suggestion on the nature and use of habits, it will be readily seen that they constitute a very important factor in a symmetrical education. Power without right habits is of comparatively little value, inasmuch as habits constitute the only medium through which power can be effectively utilized in performing work. It is also not undervaluing knowledge as one of the principal factors of an education, when it is said, that its acquisition is of much less importance in the development of a vigorous and symmetrical manhood than the acquisition of power and right habits. Too much stress, therefore, cannot be placed upon the formation of right habits as an essential part of a true education.

15. *Habits may be variously classified according to the end or purpose to be served by the classification.*

(*a*). They may be classified, for example, with reference to their source or nature into *physical* and *mental* habits, and with reference to their products or results into *general* and *special* habits.

(*b*). The following presents the classification adopted in these notes :

Habits are $\begin{cases} \text{1. Special} \\ \text{2. General} \end{cases}$ These are $\begin{cases} \text{1. Physical} \\ \text{2. Mental} \end{cases}$ $\begin{cases} (a). \text{ Intellectual} \\ (b). \text{ Moral} \\ (c). \text{ Spiritual} \end{cases}$

(*c*). Special habits will not be outlined beyond pointing out their nature and place as factors of education. Their discussion belongs properly to professional or special education, and includes a much wider range of details than is intended to be covered in these notes.

16. *A special habit may be defined as a habit which is acquired for the purpose of performing some one definite kind of work.*

(*a*). Every special work, which organs of the body or faculties of the mind are intended to perform, necessitates, for its easy and perfect performance, the acquisition of special habits or aptitudes. For example, the fingers are intended to perform, and do perform, an indefinite range of special kinds of work. But it is a well-known fact to every one, that the intelligence and will cannot make the fingers instrumental in doing finished work in any line whatsoever, until, by continued practice in doing the work, *finger-habits* are formed. When this is done, the use of the intelligence and will in directing the efforts of the fingers becomes almost entirely unnecessary. The art of knitting is a good example of this kind.

(*b*). The range of special habits is practically unlimited.   The free and effective use of every imaginable tool calls for a special habit.   The effective use, also, of each of the senses in doing special kinds of work necessitates the formation of special habits. The artist's eye, as well as his hand, if he would be a master in his department, must acquire strong and well-defined habits of seeing things as they really are, and of seeing in these things the possibilities they possess of new combinations and relations, which, when wrought out, will give rise to new forms of exquisite symmetry and beauty.

(*c*). The mind in performing its work is no less dependent upon special habits than the body. The intellectual worker, for example, who can only hold his mind to a given line of thought by a constant effort of his will, is in no better condition to do his work than the mechanic, who, by a similar effort of his will, handles his tools. Both, so long as their work is done in this way, must equally fail to produce finished results.

17. *A general habit may be defined as a habit, the exercise of which necessitates the formation of special habits, and which also of itself serves to accom-*

plish, not one but several ends, differing in their nature and purpose.

(*a*). The habit of doing well everything in the production of which the organs of the body are concerned is a good example of a general habit. This habit, it will be readily seen, affects the quality and the exercise of a wide range of special habits. For example, take the case of a mechanic in whom this habit is fully established; he will not be satisfied with acquiring imperfectly the minimum of special habits necessary for the handling of the tools of his special line of work. No, he must possess more than this. He will give himself no rest until the special habits required have reached such a degree of perfection as will enable him to perform what he undertakes in a workmanlike manner.

(*b*). The general habits which a man acquires affect not only the quality and exercise of groups of special habits which serve to perform a given work, but each of them affects in a peculiar manner the tendencies and activities of the entire man. The general habit, for example, referred to in (*a*), when fully established, will give tone and character to every kind of work to which the man possessing it may turn his attention. Should he even pass from manual to mental work, the power and influence of this habit acquired in the former will at once pass over into the latter kind of work.

(*c*). In view of the nature of *general habits* and their peculiar relation to *special habits*, their importance as a chief element in a sound education cannot be overestimated.　It is not too much, therefore, to say that to assist and wisely direct his pupils in forming right general habits is a first work of the true educator.　When this work is well done, the special habits necessary for any given line of effort will be readily formed whenever required.

The following brief outline indicates the most important general habits and their special province and use as factors of a general education.

GENERAL PHYSICAL HABITS.

18. *The habit of being constantly active under all legitimate conditions.*

(*a*). Physical activity is the result of a natural or of an induced state of the body.　The activity of most, if not all, young children is an example of the former.　The latter constitutes a habit.　A good example of this habit is found in the case of a man who, because of constant activity, has induced such a state of his body as makes him uneasy and discontented when he ceases to be engaged in active work.　When this habit is formed, everything undertaken will be executed promptly and with energy.

(*b*). This habit cannot be formed when only one line of activity is pursued.　Such a course induces just the opposite habit; namely, that of laziness.　This is illustrated very clearly in the case of professional performers of any sort.　Such performers are capable of intense activity in their chosen line.   But when not engaged in this chosen line, they find that to be active is a great burden.   They have, in fact, induced the habit of indolence or laziness.   Professional firemen, professional ball-players, etc., are examples of this sort.

19. *The habit of doing well everything in which the organs of the body are concerned.*

(*a*). This habit is usually formed through the influence of models.   For example, the child imitates the parents until he cannot do otherwise than act as they act, perform his work as they perform it.   In this case it is literally true that as the parent is, so is the child.   This peculiar influence extends to all relations of life.   But nowhere is its power shown so fully as in the case of parents and teachers.   They are the models, which are largely the determining factors in the life of all under their care.

(*b*). When this habit is fully established, it will produce uneasiness and dissatisfaction in regard to everything that is not well done, or that shows carelessness in its execution.   It will, in short, affect the execution of everything in which the body is the agent.   It will determine alike, for example, the way in which artists, mechanics, farmers, housekeepers, etc., perform their work.

20. *The habit of employing, always, the organs of the body to accomplish right and useful ends.*

(*a*). The ability to conserve and economize physical energy is certainly a very important acquisition, yet little attention is given in our educational processes to this acquisition. Hence, the literal waste of physical power in the life of almost every man is enormous. The old maxim, " Take care of the pennies, and the pounds will take care of themselves," if applied to physical energy, would yield quite as valuable results as when applied to money matters. But can it be applied ? Certainly it can, and should be. The habit of employing the physical energy which God has given us to accomplish right and useful ends can be formed just as readily as the habit of handling money in the same way. Physical energy is *capital stock* just as much as money and other property ; and more, it is the chief if not the only *capital stock* possessed by the great mass of mankind. How important, then, that a habit which will secure the right use of this universal possession should be acquired.

(*b*). When this habit is formed, it will determine very largely, if not entirely, the use that will be made of physical energy, not only in our daily work, but also in our times of recreation and amusements. Recreation and amusements are as necessary to the proper and effective use of the mind and body as food. But alas ! just as in the case of the use of food, so in this: the abuse is almost universal. Knowledge will not save men from this abuse in either case. This is evident in the matter of food and drink, for the men that know the most about both are not infrequently the victims of the greatest abuse. A confirmed habit of right living, and not knowledge, is the safeguard from this abuse. In like manner, a confirmed habit of using physical energy always for right and useful ends is the safeguard against a large share of the abuses growing out of modern recreations and amusements.

The three "General Physical Habits" to which attention has just been called, if acquired, will secure to a very large extent the proper and efficient use of the body. They constitute essential conditions, if not the only key to real success in any kind of exercise or work dependent upon the expenditure of physical energy.

GENERAL INTELLECTUAL HABITS.

The importance of forming right intellectual habits cannot be overestimated. The failure to do so makes effective intellectual effort a perpetual drudgery. The most careful supervision of the work of the young pupil is necessary to avert this result. Habits are readily formed at this time. During this period one of the most important things to accomplish is the formation of right intellectual habits. Failing to do this, whatever the pupil's intellectual ability may be, he will fail largely in using his ability effectively, and with the largest and best results. The following constitute the most important general intellectual habits to be acquired during the formative period.

21. *The habit of attention, or the power of center-*
ing mental energy upon a given subject, or of excluding
from consciousness everything which does not pertain
strictly to the subject under consideration.

(*a*). Each human being is possessed of a definite
amount of mental energy, natural (Art. 10) and acquired (Art. 11). This energy is capable of being
applied as a unit, of being completely centered upon
one definite work; or, on the other hand, it is capable of being divided and hence distributed among
several kinds of work. When the former condition
prevails, the mind exhibits its maximum power of
effort. This condition is, however, rarely if ever
reached. But the nearer it is approached, the more
effectively can mental energy be applied in performing any given work. The habit of attention is the
chief if not the only medium through which this
approach can be made, hence its formation is absolutely necessary to successful mental effort.

(*b*). This habit is, in the first place, of the nature
of a centralizing power. It operates upon the divided
elements of mental energy very much as the burning-glass operates upon the divided rays of the sun.
It brings all of these elements to a focus. And just
as combustion necessarily follows when the rays of
the sun are brought to a focus by the burning-glass,
so the analysis or decomposition of difficult complex
truths is at once accomplished when all the elements
of mental energy are brought to a proper focus by
the habit of attention.

(*c*). This habit is, in the second place, of the nature of an abstracting power, a power by which the mind withdraws itself from a conscious relation to everything but the subject under immediate consideration. This means such a state of the mind as excludes from its entire operations all that is necessarily forced upon it by its connection with the organs of sense and their environments, and also with its own past experiences. This means, in short, such a state of being as effectually closes for a time all active conscious relations between the mind and everything else, but one single absorbing subject. That such a state of being is possible, is fully certified by extreme cases of what is known as absent-mindedness.

22. *The habit of conducting observations, and, where necessary, experiments in an orderly, accurate and exhaustive manner.*

(*a*). In the earlier stages of the pupil's work too much importance cannot be attached to the formation of this habit. At that time he is naturally careless, and in haste to reach results. This tendency must be checked by impressing him with the fact that the way in which his work is done is far more important to him than results.

(*b*). Observation covers a wider range than the use of the eye. Every one of the five senses has its own field of exercises, and each should receive proper attention with reference to this habit. Observation includes, in addition to the ordinary use of the senses, their use supplemented by mechanical devices. The use of the eye, supplemented by the microscope or telescope, is an example of this kind.

(*c*). Where this habit is not formed, there is no safeguard against crude, and, in many instances, very imperfect and unwarranted conclusions being drawn from insufficient premises. Hence, without this habit, reliable and real progress in any line of investigation is impossible. This statement applies not only to the physical senses, but to all lines of investigation. The necessity of this habit in pursuing successfully and with safety investigations in language, philosophy, theology, etc., is as great as in the study of the natural sciences. Let this habit be thoroughly established during school life, and an element is fixed in the character that will prove an invaluable help and safeguard in every department of life's work.

23. *The habit of making always a diligent search for the reason, or cause of things.*

(*a*). Inquisitiveness is a marked characteristic of child life. As already stated, it lies at the root of all his mental activity. It at first demands an answer to the question, "*What is it?*" but its demand does not end here. It asks in the second place an answer to the question, "*Why is this as it is?*" This inquisitiveness, which at first is largely aimless, if properly directed, gradually grows into an intellectual habit of great value—a habit without which

science and philosophy would make but little prog
ress.

(*b*). While it is true that inquisitiveness is a common characteristic of child life, it is not true that all
can with the same readiness form this habit. Indeed,
there are many cases where, unless taken at the
right time, and handled with great skill, the formation of this habit is impossible. In such cases seien-
tific and philosophical studies can be pursued only
in a very superficial way.

24. *The habit of careful reflection, and of close self-
questioning, upon everything that is made a subject of
study, as a means of solving and explaining difficul-
tics.*

(*a*). It may be laid down as a fixed rule, that a
subject is not properly seized by the mind until reflection and close self-questioning becomes a mental
necessity. The truth of this statement will become
evident when the nature of genuine study is analyzed.

(*b*). Until this habit is formed, the student is not
in a condition to pursue successfully by himself new
courses of investigation. Nor is he even in a condition to receive the full disciplinary benefit of the
work he actually does. Reflection, meditation and
self-questioning are of the nature of a digestive process, and through this process alone can truth be
dissolved and assimilated, and made in a proper sense
a personal possession. Hence, it is of first importance that this habit should be formed at an early

stage of the student's life. In an elementary sense, very young children can form this habit.

25. *The habit of continuing every work undertaken until it is properly completed.*

(*a*). This habit when formed gives continuity and stability to every work the student undertakes. Discouragements and defeats of necessity meet every, one, not only during school life, but afterwards. The habit formed of persistently holding on to every work undertaken, until it is properly completed, is in a large measure the true solvent of these discouragements and defeats.

(*b*). If this habit is to be formed, parents and teachers must be guarded in assigning to the child or pupil such work, as he can, in view of his ability and conditioning circumstances, finish without overtaxing him. They must also be guarded not under any circumstances to accept of half-finished work. Young persons are usually just about as careless in matters of this sort as parents and teachers permit.

26. *The habit of formulating in writing, correctly and clearly, every process and result of thought before regarding such process and result as fully mastered.*

(*a*). The importance of this habit cannot be overestimated. It serves to hold the student to his work until the subject under examination is viewed from all sides, and is unified in his own mind. To be unable to commit to writing in a plain and forcible manner what has been carefully studied, is evidence that the subject is not yet fully and clearly defined in the mind.

(*b*). The formation of this habit is also of first importance, because of its practical nature. It matters not in what calling of life engaged, this habit can be turned to first-class account. A man who can put his thinking upon any subject in writing, in a clear and forcible manner, all other things being equal, has always the advantage in any department of work over those who cannot do this.

(*c*). This habit is usually found difficult to acquire. This arises chiefly from the fact that the formation of the habit is not commenced early enough, and when commenced, unnatural methods of expressing his thoughts are forced upon the pupil. If the child is taken at the right time, and trained to express in written form what he is accustomed to express orally, he will soon take real pleasure in putting in writing his oral utterances. In this way the desired habit will soon be formed, and when more advanced, the pupil will acquire the power of condensing and expressing his thinking in a clear and forcible manner.

GENERAL MORAL HABITS.

It is not what a man knows, but what he is, that determines his real course of life. In the past far too much stress has been laid by parents and teachers upon the importance of a sound knowledge of moral truths, and of the teachings of the Bible This surely is important and not to be neglected, but it is a fatal error to suppose that, where such knowledge is acquired, a young person is prepared to enter life fully assured of pursuing a true and noble course. Such knowledge, in order to secure this result, must be more than fixed formally in the memory so as to be readily recalled. It must be embodied in a well ordered course of life, that will secure the formation of permanent moral habits. Such habits will abide and exercise a controlling influence upon the life, when the knowledge acquired may fail entirely to guide and determine the course of conduct that should be pursued. The acquisition, therefore, of right moral habits is of first importance. Without such habits young persons will find it difficult, if not impossible, to maintain a blameless moral character, under the changed surroundings which they must usually encounter, when they enter upon their life work. Such habits are also as essential, as a preparation for effective moral work, as physical and intellectual habits are as a preparation for effective physical and intellectual work. In the following brief outline only such habits are given as experience has shown of real value, in maintaining a true manhood, in the midst of the traps, pitfalls and allurements of modern life.

27. The habit of rendering prompt obedience to the dictates of conscience and to the rightful commands of others.

(*a*). He that has acquired fully the power to obey, has in doing so acquired also the power to command. This is the experience of such as have risen to positions of command. They know the full power of the expression—He that has fully mastered himself is in a position, when required, to master others. Experiences of this kind emphasize very strongly the importance and practical nature of this habit.

(*b*). In seeking to guide in forming this habit, the nature of real obedience must not be overlooked. Obedience, whether we refer to the conscience or to the command of another, does not mean acts which are the products of coercion. The formal performance of what the parent, teacher or other agent may require is not necessarily obedience. The boy who does what his father or teacher may require, because the rod is held over his head, does not obey in the sense intended in this habit. Such an act is, however, sometimes wrongfully called an act of obedience. Anything short of a voluntary act should not be regarded as true obedience.

(*c*). The formation of this habit should commence at the cradle, and it should be perfected as the child passes through the development of the three periods of infancy, childhood and youth. It must be carefully noted that to obey either the dictates of conscience, or the commands of another, is comparatively easy under one set of conditions, while exceedingly difficult under another. Hence this habit can reach its perfected form only after passing through the various changing conditions supplied by these three periods of development.

(*d*). Parents and teachers not infrequently fail **in** securing the formation of this habit. This is chiefly the result of two causes. In the first place they make demands which the child cannot comply with, because of lack of sufficient physical, intellectual, or moral development. For example, it is not an infrequent occurrence for a parent or teacher to demand of an immature child a course of conduct, which they would find, even with their mature powers, difficult to pursue. But in the second place the demands made are not accompanied by the right kind of motives or stimuli to enable the child to obey. By motives or stimuli are not meant promises of rewards in the way of sweetmeats, gifts, prizes, etc., but rather rational conditions and ends, which appeal both to the conscience and reason.

28. *The habit of sincere and careful reflection upon the effects of our actions, in reference to ourselves and others, and upon the reasons that make it desirable that we should, or should not, act in any given case.*

(*a*). Sincere and careful reflection is one of the strongest safeguards against mistakes in every department of active life. But this is specially true when applied to the effects of our actions upon ourselves and others. "If I had only thought, if I had only considered, how different I would have acted," is almost the universal statement of those who fall into wrong and fatal courses of conduct. " I thought on my way and turned my feet unto thy testimonies," was the experience of the Psalmist.   This is also the usual experience of all who sincerely reflect upon the effects of their actions upon themselves and others.   How important, therefore, that this habit should be formed at an early age.

(*b*). The natural course of things in the early life of a child makes it easy to form this habit.   His first contact with the external world in which his mistakes bring to him pain and suffering forces him to reflect upon the effects of his acts upon himself.   It leads him also to consider carefully the reasons that make it desirable that he should, or should not, act.   This natural condition of things properly utilized by parents and teachers will result in forming this habit.   The child only needs to be encouraged and directed in order to become as thoughtful in regard to the effects of his actions upon others as upon himself.   He commences to be thoughtful upon what brings him suffering and pleasure through the organs of the body; but, under proper guidance, he will extend his thoughtfulness to the workings of his mind, as well as his body. This thoughtfulness may be directed by parents and teachers so as to extend to every act; in short, so that the habit may be firmly formed of never acting without sincere and careful reflection upon the consequences that may follow.

(*c*). From what has just been said, it will appear that this habit can be most readily formed during the period of infancy and childhood. For this there are several reasons, but chief among them is the fact, that all habits are most easily formed during the plastic or formative state of the particular growth with which the habit is connected. It is, therefore, all important to the future of the child that this and all other moral habits should receive attention at the right time. Neglect here is fraught with fatal consequences to the character of the future man.

29. *The habit of treating with proper regard our superiors in age, position, or ability, our equals in every respect, and our inferiors in one or more respects.*

(*a*). The great importance of this habit, its meaning and binding nature, is extensively stated in God's word: "Render therefore to all their dues: tribute to whom tribute is due; custom to whom custom; fear to whom fear; honor to whom honor. Owe no man anything, but to love one another: for he that loveth another hath fulfilled the law."

(*b*). What has been said of the formation of the preceding habit applies equally to this. "As the twig is bent the tree's inclined" is literally true here. Let the young child be taught to treat with proper regard superiors, equals and inferiors; let the habit of doing so be fixed firmly upon him, and he will, as he grows to manhood, illustrate in his life the Bible requirements in this respect.

(*c*). As the child is largely a creature of imitation, the parent and teacher must place before him, in their own conduct, a perfect example of what they want him to be and to do. It is useless to talk to the child about being respectful to others, unless the talk is accompanied by a living example. Speak to him politely, if you would have him speak to you and others politely. Treat respectfully and lovingly your equals and inferiors, if you want the child to pursue a similar course. In short, apply the golden rule to the treatment of the child as fully and as literally as in your dealings with those of mature age. Do unto the child as you would the child should do unto you, and this habit will soon become a ruling principle of the child's life.

30. *The habit of being strictly honest in dealing with ourselves, and in our dealings with others.*

(*a*). Self-deception is one of the chief causes of wrong and even criminal courses of action. The first steps of a downward course of life have their origin here. A deliberate choice of what is wrong in itself is not the usual beginning of a downward course. By a subtle process of self-deception, what is wrong is made to appear right, and hence the course of conduct that follows is justified and is considered the true one to pursue. This peculiar tendency of our nature the Bible places before us in strong and explicit terms in the following language: "The heart is deceitful above all things and desperately wicked: who can know it?" In view of this condition of things the formation of this habit is both important and difficult.

(*b*). Notwithstanding the natural difficulties which must be encountered in forming this habit, much can be accomplished if the effort to do so is commenced with infancy. There is a degree of simplicity and honesty in the ordinary child-life that makes the formation of the habit possible. This seems to be clearly implied in Christ's statement to his disciples when he says, " Verily, I say unto you, except ye be converted and become as little children, ye shall not enter into the kingdom of Heaven."

(*c*). The demand of to-day in business life, in political life, in church life, and, indeed, in family life, is transparent honesty in our dealings with ourselves and others. This demand calls for earnest and radical efforts to cultivate the formation of this habit in the family, and in our schools and colleges.

31. *The habit of doing with all our might whatever our intelligence and conscience may approve as right.*

(*a*). Half-heartedness is to be avoided in doing everything, but especially so in matters affecting our moral character. A right act or a right course of conduct should not be discounted by the way it is performed. This, however, is very commonly done. Men reason very correctly upon the most of moral questions, but they act as if they did not believe their own reasoning.

(*b*). Young children are naturally single in their aims. Their whole energy is usually applied to whatever they may have in hand.   They differ widely, however, in natural energy or force, but whatever they may possess in this respect is readily centered upon what claims present attention.   This is peculiarly true in matters approved by the intelligence and conscience.   Young children are, therefore, in the best possible condition to form this habit.   They need only proper guidance upon the part of parents and teachers, in the course of their early training, to convert this natural tendency into a strong and useful habit.

(*c*). The importance of forming this habit cannot be overestimated.   When formed, it gives character and power to everything undertaken.   It secures the confidence of all whom we may seek to serve in any way. It even disarms the criticism of those who may differ widely from us in our views of what is right and wrong. All men tacitly approve of downright earnestness in executing what the intelligence and conscience recognize as right.

THE FORMATION OF HABITS.

32. *Habits are formed by the continuous and frequent repetition, under right conditions, of the act or state by which a given end is accomplished.*

(*a*). There are three elements concerned in the formation of habits which must be carefully noted; namely, the act or state by which the proposed end can be accomplished, the intelligence which directs the act or state in accomplishing the given end, and the will power by which the act or state is produced. The process by which the habit of knitting is acquired, for example, illustrates these three factors and substantially the way in which all habits are formed. When the attempt is first made to do this work, the needles are directed every time by the use of the eye, and each motion is produced by a distinct act of the will. Both the eye and the will are so occupied at this stage with the act to be performed that attention cannot be given to anything else. By practice, however, the use both of the eye and of the will becomes less and less necessary. Finally by long and continued practice they cease to be required except to initiate the work. When this point is reached, the intelligence and will being liberated, other matters can receive attention and be freely discussed at the same time the work in hand is in progress.

(*b*). The length of the interval of time between the repetitions of an act or state is an important factor in the formation of habits. For example, it is evident that the habit of playing upon the piano can never be acquired by striking the keys in a given scale, in their proper order, an unlimited number of times, assuming that no key in the scale is touched oftener than once every ten days. It is, therefore, not repetition alone that is neccessary to form habits readily, but repetition with the interval of time between the acts reduced to its minimum.

(*c*). The repetition of the act or state involved must be consecutive. It must also, in order to produce the best effect, be continued, each time it is undertaken, as long as a normal condition of the body and mind can be maintained. The truth of this position is fully verified by experience. No habit of any sort can be acquired, within a reasonable length of time, when this condition is partially or wholly neglected. Instances of this neglect are of frequent occurrence in school work. The absence of well-conducted drill exercises, which should consist chiefly of systematic repetitions, is an example of this kind. The evil consequences of such neglect are very great, when we take into account the fact that almost every work the pupil undertakes must be reduced to a fixed habit, in order to be of practical value to him in after-life. The study of Arithmetic, Grammar, Rhetoric, Logic, etc., are familiar examples of this sort. It is true that these subjects have a practical educational value because of the mental discipline they afford. But this is not half their value. For example, the discipline acquired in gaining a knowledge of the principles and laws of Logic is important, but the power and habit of reasoning in accordance with these principles and laws, whether they are formulated as knowledge or not, is far more important. This, however, can only be acquired by doing, not by knowing. The habit of reasoning clearly and accurately is the product of persistent repetitions of acts of reasoning.

(*d*). The readiness with which a habit is formed depends upon a variety of conditions. Among these conditions may be named age, constitutional tendencies, the relation of the habit to be formed to others already formed, the exactness with which the act or state is repeated, and the intensity of the consciousness at the time of each repetition.

33. *The power and influence of habits in shaping and executing our course of life depend largely upon the conditions under which they are formed.*

(*a*). The truth of this proposition is included in the fact that any past state or experience of body or mind is capable of being reproduced in its entirety by the presence of one or more of the elements which constituted a part, in the past, either of the given state or experience, or of the conditions through which it was produced. The reproduction of past knowledge by laws of association is universally admitted. But it must be noted here that the application of these laws is not confined to the reproduction of knowledge. It is co-extensive with every state, condition and operation of the organs of the body and of the powers of the mind, whether these states, conditions and operations are conscious or unconscious.

(*b*). Keeping in mind Note (*a*), it should be observed that the conditions under which a habit is formed constitute ever afterwards the natural stimuli for its exercise. Hence the presence of one or more of these conditions necessarily tends to produce such exercise. This simple but important law of habit is fully verified in every person's experience. For example, in the case of many, walking is the condition which produces **un-**

conscious swinging of the arms, and talking vigorously, unconscious gesticulation.

(*c*). The conditions under which a habit can be acquired may be greatly varied. The habit of graceful movements of the body may be acquired in the gymnasium, in the parlor, or under the guidance, example, and instruction of the dancing master. Each of these sets of conditions may be successfully used for this purpose, but it must be noted that the conditions used determine very largely the power and influence of the habit, when formed, upon the course of life. Suppose the habit to be formed under the tuition of the dancing master, the natural stimuli, as pointed out in Note (*b*), for the exercise of the habit will then be found in such conditions as were supplied by the instructor; hence, in this case, the social and public dance will have a powerful influence upon the course of life.

(*d*). Habits of the mind, with reference to the conditions under which they are acquired, are subject to the same law as habits of the body. To illustrate, take the habit of clear and accurate reasoning. This may be acquired under very widely different conditions, indeed almost opposite conditions. In the first place, the subject matter on which the mind may work in forming the habit may be varied almost indefinitely. Mathematies pure or applied, physical sciences, language, metaphysics, or theology may each in turn, or in combination, be used for this purpose. In the second place, the teacher, the living factor, enters as a prime condition. He can vary the use of the subject matter and direct and control the work of the pupil at pleasure. But this is not all, he cannot be honest and true to himself, and do otherwise than introduce his own spirit of doing the work, as one of the most important conditions, under which his pupils form the habit. Now suppose the teacher to be an atheist, a deist, an agnostic, or, if not quite as marked a skeptic as any one of these, a practical unbeliever in God and His word, then what of the results? Such a teacher may form in his pupils the habit of clear and accurate reasoning, but this habit must be exercised, ever after, subject to *the law of the conditions under which it was acquired.* The pupil, while acquiring the habit, having been studiously exercised upon truth out of proper relation to the fountain and end of all truth, will, of course, in after-life, find pleasure and satisfaction in exercising this habit upon everything but what pertains to God and spiritual things.

(*e*). The law of the influence and power of habits illustrated in the foregoing notes is fraught with peculiar importance in reference to all educational processes. If the position enunciated can be fully verified, as we believe it can, then our course of life depends quite as much upon the way in which our education has been conducted as upon the knowledge and habits we may acquire. What we will do after our education is completed will not always be what we know to be best or right or what our habits qualify us to do, but what we are disposed to do by the change wrought in us in the act of acquiring this knowledge and these habits.

PURE AND ELEVATED TASTES.

34. *The word* TASTE *is used in several senses, which are important to note. The following should be carefully discriminated, the one from the other.*

(*a*). The word denotes the organ of sense by which we perceive through contact the *savor* of any substance. The seat of this organ is principally in the tongue.

(*b*). The word denotes the faculty of the mind by which we perceive or appreciate in objects or performances of any kind the presence or absence of symmetry, order, beauty, proportion, adaptation or excelleney of whatever sort.

(*c*). The word is used to denote the *feeling of relish* and consequent *attraction* or *repulsion* which accompanies the exercise, as defined in (*a*) and (*b*), of any organ of sense or faculty or receptivity of the the mind.

(*d*). The word taste is also used to denote the directive or constructive faculty by which our ideals of symmetry, order, beauty, etc., are realized.

35. *The range of our tastes is coextensive with our entire being.*

(*a*). Tastes are natural and acquired. Each human being commences life in the possession of certain natural or inherited tastes. These natural tastes assert themselves from the dawn of life onwards. Their influence even in infancy is very marked. The child of only a few years frequently manifests an extraordinary taste for a certain line of physical or mental activity. Some, for example, show such a taste for music, others for drawing, others for natural history, others for investigating the why and wherefore of everything, others for certain amusements, others for certain courses of conduct both good and bad, others, in short, for the exercise of some one or more of the possible natural activities or receptivities of the body and mind. So much for some of the facts in regard to natural tastes ; let us now note acquired tastes.

(*b*). The range of acquired tastes is much greater than that of the natural. There is no active or receptive power of body or mind in connection with which a taste cannot be acquired. The truth of this statement is easily verified by experiment. Few, if any, have failed to observe how readily tastes of every sort are formed. Even states of the body and of the mind which at first are very trying and offensive, may, by persistent effort, become enjoyable and finally result in an overmastering taste. The use of tobacco is a familiar example of this sort. In most cases the first use of it produces very unpleasant experiences, yet by persistent use these unpleasant experiences are entirely overcome, and a taste is formed so strong that it is almost unconquerable. The law illustrated by this example holds true of every active and receptive power of the body and mind. The continuous exercise of such powers, under proper conditions, results invariably in forming a relish or taste for such exercise.

36. *Our tastes have a powerful influence in the formation of our character, and in determining our social condition and the manner in which we perform our life work.*

(*a*). Our tastes largely make and unmake us. They are the secret springs which, to a great extent, if not entirely, shape both our private and public life. But few, if any, are fully conscious of the peculiar and subtle influence of their tastes in determining their sphere of work, the manner in which they perform their work, their recreations and amusements, their social and religious associations, their companionships, their reading and study, their interest in the well-being of others, in short, their real character, and their place in the world. Say what we will, our likes and dislikes have an untold influence in shaping our lives. And what are these likes and dislikes but the direct products of our tastes either natural or acquired?

(*b*). The powerful influence of taste is felt not only among those who give themselves up to degrading practices, but also among the most refined and educated classes. It is the principal channel through which extravagances and vices of all sorts are introduced into social life and even into literary circles. When the tastes, social, literary or otherwise, of any community are vitiated, the flood-gates of destructive influences are thrown wide open. It is said that " knowledge is power." This may be so; but knowledge is very weakness in the presence of natural and acquired tastes. The power of knowledge, and even of reason and sound judgment, vanishes before the power of our tastes like the morning dew before the rising sun. Physicians, for example, tell us of the destructive consequences of the diet so commonly served upon our tables, and we may sincerely believe them. But what of that, our tastes will have the mastery. They are stronger than our knowledge, reason and judgment. We will indulge, even although the fatal consequences of a wrecked physical constitution stare us in the face, or have already been partially experienced.

(*c*). Taste, as the faculty by which beauty, symmetry, etc., are perceived and appreciated, is the key to success in every line of productive effort. The mechanic, the artist, and the literary man are equally dependent upon the use of this key. It is, in the first place, a powerful incentive to all true effort. But it does not stop here. It is the only force which shapes and directs the exercise of physical and mental power in performing work. It is the inspiration which gives perfection of finish alike to the products of the artisan, the artist, the rhetorician, and the poet. Without the existence and exercise of a well-trained taste, there can be no master-mechanics, artists, or rhetoricians. It is taste that decorates the palace and transforms the humble home into a place of comfort, neatness and beauty. Taste constitutes the principal factor in determining our course of life and molding our character.

In short, a man never is, and cannot **be, an** effective worker in any sphere of life **for** which **he is not** fitted by natural or acquired tastes.

37. *It is the imperative duty of parents and teachers to provide the right conditions for the 'formation of pure and elevated tastes, in view of their powerful influence on life and character.*

(*a*). The intelligent discharge of this duty makes **it** important to have a clear view of the primary conditions affecting the formation of tastes, hence the following suggestions on his subject should be carefully noted.   Tastes, with reference to their formation, may be classified as follows:

(1). Tastes, where there is a constitutional tendency towards forming them.

(2). Tastes, where there is no constitutional tendency either towards or against forming them.

(3). Tastes, where there is a constitutional antagonism to forming them.

Each of these classes of tastes must, **in** reference to their formation and exercise, be again resolved into two classes; namely, *Active Tastes* and *Passive Tastes.*   By active tastes are meant those tastes whose exercise is connected with an active state of the mind or of the body.   A taste for geometrical reasoning, or for scientific investigation, is an example of a taste for an active state of the mind; and a taste for out-door sports, such as ball-playing, for an active state of the body.   By passive tastes are meant those tastes whose exercise is connected with a passive state either of the mind or of the body. A taste for seclusion or solitude is an example of the former, and a taste for the effects of a narcotic, such as tobacco, or of an alcoholic stimulant, such as brandy, is an example of the latter

(*b*). Here it should be noted that the real object, in every instance, which fascinates, attracts, or for which a taste is formed, is a mental or subjective state. This subjective state has, however, invariably connected with it what may be called an external object. This external object is in a certain sense the occasion or cause of the subjective state, and hence it is usually improperly regarded as the real object of the taste. To make this point clear, take the example given above of a taste for geometrical reasoning. Here it will be observed that the diagrams, symbols, difficulties, and results constitute the external object whose presence is necessary to produce the state of mind for which there is such a strong relish, fascination or taste. It will also be observed that this external object is sought and its leadings followed, in the face of great difficulties, not for the sake simply of the knowledge that may be gained, but because it has in it that which produces states of mind that are fascinating. These states of mind are the real objects of the relish or taste which forces the person on in the study of geometry, even in the face of great obstacles and privations. The principle illustrated by this example applies to passive as well as to active tastes. Narcotics and alcoholic stimulants are sought, notwithstanding their injurious consequences, simply because **of** the taste formed for the mental states which their use necessarily produces.

(*c*). The external object and the subjective or real object of taste sustain to each other a relation which should be carefully noted. In passive tastes this relation is peculiar and very marked. Indeed, it is so constant that it properly deserves to be called a law. Bearing in mind, that a taste as shown in (*b*), is an attraction for a state of mind which yields a certain degree of pleasure during its continuance, this law may be stated as follows :

To maintain uniformity in the degree of pleasure experienced from a given passive state of mind, there must be at every repetition of this state an increase of the quantity or intensity of the external stimuli which are the occasion or cause of the given state.

The workings of this law, in passive states which depend upon stimuli supplied through the body, may be illustrated by the use of alcoholic and narcotic stimulants. It takes, for example, but a teaspoonful of whiskey, at first, to produce a pleasurable state of mind. But if the same degree of pleasure is to be produced an indefinite number of times, the quantity of whiskey taken must be gradually increased. The wineglass-full must soon take the place of the teaspoonful. And, finally, if the effort to experience the same degree of pleasure is to be made even approximately successful, spiced whiskey must soon take the place of the pure article, as increase of quantity gradually ceases to produce the desired effect. The use of tobacco and other narcotics follows the same law. At first a change of quantity, as in the case of the alcohol, regulates the degree of pleasure, but in the course of time the strong cigar and the old saturated pipe are decidedly preferred.

(*d*). The principle illustrated by these examples holds true also of passive states which are dependent for their existence upon stimuli supplied through the mind. The printed page and other similar sources furnish material which is taken directly into the mental organism, as readily as whiskey is taken into the physical organism. The mind is frequently as effectually injured by the indulgence of tastes formed through stimuli supplied in this way as the body by physical stimuli. As an example of this, the destructive effects upon the mind of a certain kind of light reading, which ministers chiefly, if not entirely, to the indulgence of passive states, is only paralleled by the destructive effects of alcohol and narcotics upon the body. This is easily verified by reference to the downward career of boys and girls who, perhaps under the guidance of fond mothers, have formed strong tastes for passive states by the reading of passional stories in Sunday-school books. These stories may, for a time, serve the purpose of ministering to the tastes being formed; but, as in the ease of the alcohol, the pleasure they supply must gradually diminish unless the stimuli they contain are gradually increased. The Sunday-school passional stories must therefore grad-

ually give place to others possessed of stronger passional elements.   These, in turn, must give way to
stories spiced with the wild adventures of reckless lives,
and, finally, these again to stories of the lowest grade,
spiced with the crimes of even abandoned characters.

(*e*). The foregoing illustrations are sufficient to call
attention to the important nature of the relation, in
the case of passive states, existing between the external
and real object of taste.   It must, however, be carefully noted that this relation, while making possible, as
has been pointed out, the most degrading and destructive consequences, makes possible, on the other
hand, the most elevating and ennobling products of the
human soul.   The highest products of the artisan and
the artist are alike debtors to this relation.   The musician, the painter, the sculptor, the poet and the orator
are alike inspired by this relation to seek constantly
higher and yet higher expressions of the external objects of taste, that they may supply the conditions which
produce the higher subjective pleasures which their
tastes demand.

(*f*). It should here be carefully noted that the relation of the external object of taste to the subjective object, in active states of mind, differs materially from what
has been pointed out regarding passive states.   In active
states uniformity in the pleasure experienced, at every
repetition of them, is maintained without necessarily in-
creasing the quantity or intensity of the external stimuli. ·Ball-playing is a familiar example of this.   The
boy here experiences the same, if not a greater, degree

of pleasure as he resorts, again and again, to the same unchanged round of external conditions, to produce the physical activity which is the source of his pleasure. The principle illustrated by ball-playing holds equally true of pleasures experienced from active states of mind which are dependent for their existence upon external conditions which are the products of mind alone. The degree of pleasure, therefore, which accompanies an active state of body or mind, remains uniformally the same, or is increased in each repetition of the state, so long as the external stimuli are unchanged. This is not true, as has been pointed out, of passive states. In passive states the degree of pleasure diminishes in each repetition unless the quantity or intensity of the external stimuli is increased. The general principle, therefore, which appears to prevail, in reference to the repetition of active and passive states of body or of mind, may be briefly stated thus:

The external conditions and stimuli remaining unchanged, active states STRENGTHEN *and passive states* WEAKEN *by repetition.*

The bearing of this general principle, upon the importance of rightly directing the pupil in the formation of pure and elevated tastes, will be apparent from the illustrations given in the foregoing notes.

(*g*). In reference to the threefold classification of tastes given in (*a*), the following hints should be carefully noted:

First. Acquired tastes are invariably the products of the persistent and continued exercise of some activity or passivity of the body or of the mind. The exercise by which a taste is formed may be either voluntary or compulsory; hence the classification into *voluntary* and *compulsory* tastes. Voluntary tastes originate, usually, in a natural tendency or in a desire to gratify an ambition of some sort, or to be fitted to accomplish a certain work or end. Compulsory tastes, on the other hand, originate invariably in a desire to be fitted to accomplish certain ends, or in circumstances over which the person forming them has no control. The quality, strength and permanency of each taste formed depend upon constitutional tendencies and the conditions under which it has been formed.

Second. Natural tendencies exist towards wrong tastes as well as right tastes. In either case, however, the law of formation is the same. They are formed, and made effective in shaping conduct and character, simply by providing a constant supply of the conditions which will secure the persistent exercise of the activity or passivity of the body or of the mind with which each taste stands connected. These conditions are remarkably variable. A boy, for example, may be forced to form the impure taste of chewing tobacco on account of his special companions, social surroundings, or of some imagined good effect upon an ailment with which he is much troubled, etc. These conditions are largely, if not entirely, during the periods of infancy, childhood and youth, under the control of parents and teachers, hence their great responsibility for the future conduct and character of those committed to their care.

Third. In the case of tastes towards which there is no natural tendency, the first thing to be done is **to** create a tendency. This is accomplished by supplying, in the right way, the conditions that will **necessi**tate the activity in connection with which the taste is to be formed. A taste, for example, for the reading of a certain class **of** books, can readily be created, **by** conditioning the pupil so that he appreciates the ne · cessity of such reading, for the accomplishment of certain ends which he regards as very desirable. At first the reading, in such a case, is performed as a dry and unavoidable duty. In time, however, pleasure begins to accompany the discharge of the duty, and finally, by persistency, a strong taste for the exercise is developed. This illustrates the course that must usually be followed in the formation of tastes of this class. Practically, the same course must be pursued in the formation of tastes to which there is a natural antagonism. The variation in the appliances that must be adopted to secure the formation of tastes of this and the other class will be suggested by the special conditions and requirements in each case, and by the good judgment and tact of parents and teachers.

Fourth. As in the case of habits there are *general tastes* which necessitate the formation of a certain class of *special tastes*. A strong taste, for example, for social enjoyment is one of this kind. Its existence necessarily leads to the formation of *special tastes* to which it may be even naturally antagonistic, but without which the associations cannot be formed by which it can be fully satisfied. A correct and full appreciation of this principle is of first importance to parents and teachers. Their's is the duty of directing in the formation of *general tastes* which will necessitate *special tastes* that are pure and elevating, and that will result in the formation of a noble character and a consistent and effective life. Among these general tastes may be named: A taste for genuine work, physical, intellectual, moral and spiritual; a taste for reading standard works, books which require earnest and continued study to appreciate fully what they contain; and a taste for social enjoyments which minister to a pure and symmetrical development of mind, heart and body.

ACQUISITION OF KNOWLEDGE.

38. *The acquisition of knowledge is not the principal end to be sought in a true and liberal education.*

(*a*). The truth of this proposition is perhaps theoretically accepted, yet in practice it is almost universally denied. This may be easily verified by observing carefully the work done in our schools and colleges and the tests applied to show that the work required has been performed. The ability to pass examinations for promotion and honors does not, for example, depend upon the fine character the pupils have formed under the guidance of their teachers; nor upon the acquisition of habits and tastes by which the power and knowledge acquired can be rightly utilized and made to serve the highest good of the pupils themselves and of humanity. These are not the qualifications which will secure the highest honors in examinations as they are usually conducted. Not unfrequently do the highest honors go to members of classes lacking in all of these qualifications, simply because knowledge alone is made the basis upon which such honors are bestowed. This is a great evil which must be corrected before our schools and colleges can yield the best and highest results. This correction cannot, however, be made so long as teachers and others regard the acquisition of knowledge as the principal end of a liberal education.

(*b*). A large waste of the pupils' time and energy is made in cramming into the memory useless details for passing equally useless examinations. Teachers know right well that in six months or a year, after these examinations have been passed, the details, which cost such great effort to acquire, must inevitably disappear from the mind. This is particularly true of the endless details which pupils are usually compelled to acquire in such subjects as arithmetic, grammar, geography, etc. The defence for this cramming process, in the face of the fact that these details pass so soon from the mind, is the mental discipline which the work performed affords. This, however, is a great mistake. No such mental discipline as is assumed is afforded. The act of acquiring knowledge which serves this end must be real and not simply apparent as in this case. It must mean, not the cramming of forms and symbols into the memory, but the placing of the mind in actual conscious relations to existing entities, realities and phenomena. It must mean real personal experiences of what is and not merely of the forms and symbolism, which serve only to call what is into consciousness. This, however, is not always required to pass successfully, what appear to be, very formidable examinations. These can be passed by simply fixing in the memory, for the time being, what some text-book or lecturer has said upon the subject. Questions pertaining to the most profound problems in science, philosophy and language may thus be apparently answered, while the persons giving the answers may have failed, in any true sense, to construe in consciousness the realities which enter into, and constitute the very essence of these problems. This condition of things grows largely out of the wrong conception, which commonly prevails, in regard to the true nature of knowledge and of the function of words.

39. *A knowledge of words as mere sounds or written forms is in no sense a knowledge of the realities which they are intended to represent.*

(*a*). Knowledge involves three things: a *being* who knows, an *object* known, and a *consciousness* of a *determinate relation* between the being and the object. The consciousness of this determinate relation constitutes what may be called subjective knowledge. The word knowledge, it must here be noted, is also used in an objective sense to denote conscious experiences which have been associated with words or other symbols by which they are recalled, at any time, into present consciousness. Knowledge in this sense can be preserved for future use in the form of books and other records. These books and records are, however, available only to persons who have experienced the elementary consciousnesses represented by the words.

(*b*). It must here be observed that words are, in a strict sense, simply representative in their use. They serve only as the means of recalling into consciousness experiences with which they were associated in a former act of consciousness. An apparent exception to this statement must be carefully noted. The sound or written form which is called a word, in any language, may itself be the object known in an act of knowledge. In this case the sound or written form ceases to be a word, and is simply an object of knowledge, in the same sense as any other sound or drawing can be, or even a tree or article of furniture. The sole object of consciousness here is the sound or written form. No knowledge is acquired, in any sense, of the object which the sound or written form represents when used as a word. What is true of words, in this respect, is equally true of sentences, paragraphs, and entire discourses. A person, for example, having no knowledge whatever of the representative power of Latin words, may fix in the memory Latin sentences, paragraphs and discourses just as well as words. The former may require a little more effort than the latter, but it can be readily done.

When done, however, just as in the case of the single word, the only object of consciousness or knowledge, before the mind, is simply the combinations of sounds or characters fixed in the memory.

(*c*). It will further be observed from the position stated in Notes (*a*) and (*b*) that no new knowledge can be communicated by the use of words only, except in the sense of new combinations of the knowledge acquired from the objects, entities or realities of which the mind has already been conscious. The correctness of this view is evident from the office of words. As already suggested, whether spoken or written, they are only signs which serve to recall into consciousness a certain number of ideas, objective realities or experiences which by common consent or otherwise have been associated with them, during the period in which they have been used. Words, therefore, perform their legitimate function when they serve simply as signs to call into consciousness one or more of the realities with which they have been thus associated. A correct and complete knowledge, also, of the meaning of a word consists in a clear apprehension of all of the actual realities which it has served at any time to call into human consciousness. The study of the meaning of words, therefore, as such, properly conducted, consists in tracing and experiencing the actual consciousness of which they are now or have been at any time signs.

40. *The educational process, rightly conducted, will*

invariably give to the pupil possession of systematized knowledge.

(*a*). The expression *systematized knowledge* is used in this proposition in two senses, which must be carefully noted. It is used, first, to denote the knowledge which the pupil himself has traced back to the general truths and principles on which it rests, and which, after doing this, he has arranged in orderly form and fixed permanently in his mind. This may be designated *scientific knowledge*, whether it pertains to language, philosophy, theology, science or art. The expression, in the second place, is used to denote the knowledge of the productive or causative relation of things which the pupil discovers in pursuing his other work, and which he arranges also in orderly form and utilizes for practical ends. This may be designated *working knowledge*. The method by which the result, included in both of these senses, is reached will be noted under the head of *Principles of Pupils' Work*.

(*b*). The first meaning noted in (*a*) applies to all of the pupil's work. Systematized knowledge in this sense is always the product of well-directed efforts upon the part of the pupil. In order, however, that these efforts may secure the best results, he must be allowed, in every subject, to work with what may be called raw material. It is in the act of analyzing and reducing to order and system this raw material that true mental discipline is acquired. Where this kind of work is not done it is impossible to secure the highest order of results in this respect.   In this work there are two steps which must be noted.   A subject may be carefully analyzed and each truth of which it is composed discovered, clearly defined, and assigned its proper place in the system of truths of which it is one. This is the first step towards acquiring systematized knowledge, and it is a very important step, but, taken alone, incomplete.   It agrees, in a marked way, with *digestion*, or the first step in preparing food for the nourishment and development of the body.   In the case of the body, digestion may be completed, but physical development is not secured until the matter thus made ready is distributed and disappears in the living organism through the action of assimilation. In like manner new truths may be analyzed and clearly apprehended, but until, by a similar process of assimilation, they are united to the body of truth already in possession of the mind, and have thus taken their proper place in connection with the mental organism, they fail to yield to the pupil their true and highest benefit.   The process by which this is accomplished is the second step in acquiring systematized knowledge covered by the first meaning noted in (*a*).

(*c*). The second meaning noted in (*a*) has reference to a knowledge of the relations between means and end, cause and effect, etc., and the right use of these in the economy of life.   A pupil may master a subject thoroughly as a system of connected truths, and yet fail signally in being able to utilize, in a practical way, the truths he has thus mastered.   This failure, however, does not imply that the pupil has not gained a clear and perhaps exhaustive knowledge of the subject, regarded simply as a system of related truths. Instances, in proof of this, can be given without number. A pupil, for example, may acquire such a knowledge of the elements of geometry. He may be able, in this way, to pass a rigid examination on the entire subject, of the sort which calls for nothing beyond the truths and principles involved in a series of logical demonstrations, and yet he may fail largely, if not entirely, in utilizing these truths and principles, in a productive way, as means to an end.

(*d*). The nature and extent of the systematized knowledge the pupil should acquire, during each period of the educational process, will be outlined under the head of *Principles of Pupils' Work.*

PERIODS OF DEVELOPMENT.

In the following outline, of the three natural periods of human development, attention is called only to the more important facts which affect the course that should be pursued by parents, teachers and others intrusted with the education of the young. These facts, however, if carefully noted, will greatly assist in making clear the principles and laws of physical and mental development already outlined and which will be hereafter presented.

PERIOD OF INFANCY.

This period extends from birth to about the end of the seventh year, and is marked by the peculiar conditions and changes set forth in the following propositions :—

41. *The infant commences the solution of the problem of life with a body and mind inherited from his parents.*

(*a*). Each infant commences life with a physical constitution inherited from his parents. This constitution, and this alone, must be the starting-point of all physical growth. Hence this must determine and regulate, in the first place, the conditions, including the supply of food, with which the infant should be provided, through the agency of the parent and teacher, to produce a healthy and vigorous physical organism.

(*b*). It is now generally conceded by the best authorities that the infant inherits from his parents a wide range of aptitudes. At birth he is in possession of a definite individuality which distinguishes him from all other children. This individuality includes physical powers which necessarily develop a body containing the characteristic features of one or both parents. It also includes physical and mental powers and aptitudes, which as surely as in the case of the features of the face, when unrestrained, will manifest mental power and produce a course of action containing the characteristic power and actions of one or both parents.

(*c*). The infant commences life with an extremely plastic nature, capable of being molded and directed almost as the parent or teacher may choose. This condition of things makes it possible to remove, largely, constitutional or inherited deformities, and to transform, if not to annihilate entirely, powers and aptitudes which, if left unchanged, would develop into a defective if not vicious character.

42. During the first four years of the period of infancy, the child is dependent entirely upon the parents for his objective surroundings and treatment; hence the following duties are imperative upon the parents:

(*a*). The parent should furnish proper physical conditions for the healthy growth of the child's body. These conditions include at least the following: A proper supply, at right intervals of time, of nutritious food; an abundant supply of pure air; the free application of pure water upon every part of the body; clothing of the right kind to protect every part of the body from injurious exposure, and which admits a free and healthful exercise of all its organs; constant and judicious outdoor exercises, in which the feet, the hands and other organs are actively used; and plenty of undisturbed rest and sleep. These conditions should be carefully supplied throughout the growing period of the child's life. But the absence of them during infancy, and especially the first four years, results in greater evil than at any other time.

(*b*). The parent should furnish proper conditions for mental growth. These conditions include at least the following : Such contact with natural and artificial objects as will produce a healthful activity of all the senses ; such help, in the form of example, as will lead the child to use words correctly in expressing his own actual experiences ; such exercise and guidance as will enable him to form the habit of using his feet, his hands, his mouth, and other organs of the body in a proper manner ; and such precepts and examples also as will cause him to exercise constantly his moral and spiritual nature.

43. *During the period of infancy the peculiar process of physical and mental growth that is going on demands special care in the treatment of the child.*

(*a*). About the end of the seventh year the brain reaches nearly its full size, while the other organs of the body have little more than commenced their growth. The imperfect condition of the brain during this period, coupled with its rapid growth, unfits it for continuous work. In this connection it should be carefully noted that all physical as well as mental activity is the direct product of brain-work. Hence, to save the brain from overwork, the greatest care must be taken to guard the child against undue physical as well as mental activity.

(*b*). Physical activity is the natural and necessary

product of **the** growing process going on in the body, coupled with the endless variety of **new** experiences which contact with the external world **brings** to the child. Hence any course of treatment **of** the child, either in or **out** of the school which prevents **un-duly** this activity, subverts a necessary condition of growth which will prove fatal to the natural and successful development of the body and of the mind. It is, therefore, clearly the duty of both parents **and** teachers to guide, not to prevent, this activity.

44. *The period of infancy is marked by certain characteristics which should determine the course of the parents and teacher in training the body and mind.*

These characteristics include the following:

(*a*). The judgment, reason, will, or conscience plays but a very small part in controlling the child's actions. The activity, therefore, of the senses, and consequently of the mind, is the product of a condition of the sensory organs which may properly be called hunger. Sense-food is demanded, and must be had without much regard to kind or quantity. The child pursues in this the same reckless and indiscriminate course as he does in supplying the demands of the stomach. Hence the parent and teacher must guide this intense sense-hunger, and furnish the proper conditions and surroundings for its healthful exercise and development.

(*b*). Inquisitiveness lies at the root of all mental activity. This powerful inherent tendency of our nature manifests itself in two forms : *first*, in constantly asking the question, *What is it ?* and *second*, in pressing the question, *Why is it as it is ?*   The first is a demand for knowledge ; the second, for the principles and reasons of things.   The child's inquisitiveness is almost exclusively of the first form, and is the natural product of the sense-hunger before mentioned.   Unless this is blunted by unnatural treatment, he will insist upon knowing everything just as it is.   He will continue to look at, to taste, to smell, to handle the objects that come within his reach, until they cease to yield him any more new sense-food.   Then he will show the same restlessness and uneasiness which accompany the lack of a proper supply of food for the stomach.

(*c*). The child's actions are aimless in the sense of not containing any plot or plan which reaches beyond what is now and here.   In short, they are aimless in the singleness of their aim.   The child literally complies with the precept, " Take no thought for the morrow," hence the singleness and intensity of his activities.   He loses himself entirely in what is now and here.   If, for example, he is crying, he is all crying; if playing, he is all playing.   This characteristic of child-nature, properly utilized by parents and teachers, acts as one of the most powerful elements in forming a simple, pure and strong character.

(*d*). Simple credulity is a natural condition of infant life.   Everything is to the child what it appears to be. He is not disposed to doubt his senses, nor does he take any account of the endless variety of conditions that may give a false coloring to what is present to the sense or mind. Also, in making his own experience the measure by which he judges others, he necessarily takes for granted that the statements and reports of his seniors, of experiences that lie beyond his, are of the same truthful character as his own. Hence he accepts of them without any questioning, until, as he grows older, he establishes by unpleasant experiences their untruthfulness. When he reaches this conclusion, a new condition of things breaks in upon him, and he gradually commences to doubt almost everything that has not been tested by himself. This process has its beginning in the period of infancy, is intensified in childhood, and reaches its worst form in youth. In view of the natural consequences of the abuse of this characteristic of infant-nature, it should be a fixed principle of both parents and teachers never under any circumstances to deceive a child.

(*e*). During this period each organ of the body is in the most plastic state. Coupled with this, there is intense physical activity and absolute singleness of aim. All the physical and mental power of the child is present in every separate course of action in which he engages. Hence the readiness with which his activities can be transformed into habits. The importance of this characteristic of infant-nature cannot be over-estimated. It is capable of being used for evil as well as for good. This is illustrated in the formation of what are known as loafing habits, including the awkward use of feet and hands and other organs of the body. But it is especially illustrated in the formation of habits of disobedience to parents and others having rightful authority, and of disrespect of law and of the just claims of superiors in age and in experience. Habits of this kind are largely formed during the period of infancy. Hence at this time neither parent nor teacher should fail to give proper attention to this element of the child's nature.

PERIOD OF CHILDHOOD.

This period commences about the seventh year of the child's life, and ends between the twelfth and sixteenth. Surroundings, climate, health, and other causes produce an unnaturally rapid development of the body and mind, and hence children pass from the second to the third period at different times between the ages named. An early change from the second to the third period is not desirable. The longer the spirit and simplicity of childhood continues, unimpaired by a vigorous activity of body and mind, the greater the promise of a strong and vigorous manhood and wo-manhood.

The following propositions suggest questions demanding the attention of parents and teachers during this period.

45. *The brain, sensory organs, and mechanical organs have reached a degree of maturity which demands a wider range of sports or physical exercises than during infancy.*

(*a*). **An** increase of physical energy is a necessary product of the process of healthful growth. This energy during childhood increases more rapidly than it can be used in the ordinary activity of the body, hence the demand for an outlet. Play or sport is the only natural outlet. Work can in no way be made a substitute. This is evident from the very nature of play and work. In play the primary end sought is the pleasure or enjoyment present in the very acts performed, while in work the primary end sought is always a useful result outside of the acts performed. In work the present experience may be pleasant or painful. The activity is continued, not as in play because of present physical enjoyment, but because of the influence of some outside power, and hence is not the natural demand of the growing organism. Then, again, surplus physical energy is generated in every organ of the body; but work, from the very nature of the case, affords an outlet only for the energy generated in certain mechanical organs, such as the foot, the hand, etc., and hence in the formative condition of the body tends, unless carefully guarded, to destroy the symmetrical development of its organs.

(*b*). The natural discharge of surplus physical energy is always accompanied by present pleasurable sensations. This discharge takes place only through the exercise of the organs in which the energy is generated; hence the necessity of the endless variety of activity characteristic of the child. He runs, walks, jumps, rolls, tumbles, twists the body into all possible shapes, talks, laughs, shouts, and makes all kinds of noises; in short, if left to himself and surrounded by proper conditions, he discharges surplus physical energy at every pore of the body. This is the necessary accompaniment of a healthful physical growth. Hence, any system of education, which does not make proper provision for the natural discharge of physical energy, can never build up strong and symmetrical men and women.

(*c*). The nature and character of sports change with the growth of the body and mind. During infancy and a large portion of childhood, the pleasurable sensations accompanying the discharge of physical energy is almost the child's sole reason for engaging in sports. Hence the same sport or the same round of movements continues to be repeated consecutively, until, through the exhaustion of surplus energy, this pleasurable sensation ceases to be produced. It only requires, however, a short time to restore this exhausted energy; hence the child returns again to the same sport with as much zest as before. The fact that the physical energy generated in the various organs of the child's body is quickly exhausted and as quickly restored, is the reason of the peculiar delight which he takes in a rapid succession of different sports which call into exercise constantly new combinations of his organs. In this connection it should be observed that, as the mental powers of the child commence to control his action—as he commences to feel an ambition to excel—his sports become more complex and continuous, and less of the nature of pure, spontaneous, physical exercise, and less productive of real good to the child. Indeed, purely ambitious considerations may control to such an extent as to convert what may be called a sport into an exhaustive and injurious work.

(*d*). No physical exercises are productive of such healthful results as those which are spontaneous and free from all constraint. Hence, plays and sports conducted in a well-regulated playground rank first among physical exercises. " Order in confusion," and proper regard to the rights of the weak and the strong, should be the only requirements of such a playground. No scheme of regulating the sports should be adopted that will deprive the children of the delightful experiences consequent only upon a free and spontaneous activity of the organs of the body. It is very clear, however, that every school is not, and perhaps cannot be, provided with proper aecommodations for outdoor sports; hence resort must be had to calisthenic exercises as the next best thing that can be done. For disciplinary purposes, and to promote graceful movements of the body and the development of special organs, calisthenic exercises have a decided advantage over the other. Yet they fail to infuse into the body and mind that vitalizing and healthful power which results from free exercise in the open air; hence calisthenics should always have, where the other is possible, the second place in the physical exercises connected with a school.

46. *The child, during this period, associates indiscriminately with other children of his own age, and is easily affected by their language, actions and habits.*

(*a*). The distinction of sex has but slight influence in determining the child's associates during this period. The same natural impulses regulate the general conduct of both boys and girls. The natural promptings and attractions of their physical natures are the same. Hence they enjoy, unless warped by conditions imposed by the parents, the same plays and sports. These plays and sports bring to both the same intense pleasure. This state of things should not be disturbed by artificial requirements imposed in obedience to the supposed demands of society. In this period of child-life, boys and girls should be allowed the same freedom of outdoor sports, and should, under proper restrictions, mingle freely with each other.

(*b*). If left to his own natural impulses, the influence of occupation, position, or rank in life, and so on, is almost entirely disregarded by the child in choosing his associates. Pleasure or enjoyment is the chief thing sought in his companions, and this pleasure comes to him during this period chiefly through the exercise of his physical organs. Hence he selects as his associates, without much regard to anything else, those who can minister most freely to this exercise. If he enjoys special field sports, his companions will be such as can contribute most to this enjoyment. It matters little what they are socially or morally; the boys from the lowest stratum of society are valued as companions in those field sports just as much as those from a higher plane. This natural forgetfulness of all social distinctions accompanied with the strong tendency to form habits, is one of the most powerful elements for good or evil in child-nature. Properly directed, it will build up a broad and noble manhood, which will always exercise sympathy for all classes and conditions of men. But if left unguided, **it** usually, as society is now constituted, leads the child into wrong courses of action, and fixes upon **him** habits which affect injuriously his whole life. Hence the importance upon the part of parents and teachers of a careful study of this phase of child-life. Hence, also, the importance of the most earnest effort to surround the child with such conditions as will rightly guide him in his necessary associations with other children, and in the choice of his companions.

47. During this period the activity of the senses continues, and is accompanied by the development of reflection, and hence of the simplest form of reasoning and of search for the causes of material and immaterial phenomena.

(*a*). The child touches, tastes, smells and handles everything that comes within his reach, and he cannot do otherwise if he follows the impulses of his nature. These natural impulses should not be put under chains. The child should be left free, and indeed encouraged to apply all his senses in examining into the nature of his surroundings. To do otherwise is to crush out of him what God designed as one of the most important elements of a strong intellectual and moral nature. There is but one course in this matter. The senses should be gratified, and their exercises guided in such a manner as to form the power and habit of making accurate observations. This cannot be done either by leaving the child free to use all his senses indiscriminately as chance may direct, or by cramping him at once into a scientific mold where the most orderly use is made of each sense. The power and habit of using the senses accurately is a growth—is the product of a gradual and natural transformation of the inherent sense-hunger in a child—is a necessary working force. The simple duty, then, of both parents and teachers, is to supply the necessary conditions to produce this transformation.

(*b*). Reasoning, reflection and search for the causes of things, in their simplest forms, commence with the very first dawn of intelligence ; but during infancy the imperfect condition of the brain and nervous system, and the strong demand made upon this imperfect organism by the process of growth, and by the endless variety of new objects presented to the senses, excludes the possibility of reasoning and reflection proper. During infancy, however, the child usually exhausts the enjoyment afforded by simple sports and by the simple use of his senses upon surrounding objects. Hence, in order to have new enjoyments, he is naturally compelled to form new combinations in his sports, and to seek new objects on which to exercise his senses. This condition of things, therefore, makes a demand for a higher order of reasoning and reflection than was necessary during infancy. In this connection it should be carefully noted that the process of reasoning and reflection belonging to childhood is of a concrete nature, and pertains to such subjects and principles as can be illustrated or demonstrated objectively. Hence the course of study during childhood should be confined to what is concrete and experimental.

48. *The child lives in the present; his actions are almost entirely the products of present attractions and repulsions, of present simple convictions of right and wrong, or of habits already formed.*

(*a*). The attractions and repulsions which control the child's actions during infancy and the earlier part of childhood pertain largely to the senses. What gives sentient pleasure or pain usually decides the course of action. Hence, the system of rewards and punishments so commonly adopted in controlling the child's will. Intellectual attractions and repulsions gradually rise into prominence. As the child enters the period of youth, they have a strong influence upon his actions. His volitions gradually become more the products of reason and forethought. His convictions of right and wrong, however, continue to be largely the products of simple principles, wrought into his mind by his parents and teachers during infancy and childhood. When a demand for action is made upon him, these principles rise into consciousness and determine the course to be pursued.

(*b*). All motives which influence the will are states of consciousness—such as emotions, feelings and perceptions of utility, propriety, right and wrong, and so on—which are present at the time the will is to be. exercised. These states of consciousness may be either the products of our immediate present surroundings and hence transitory, or they may be the products of past experiences, principles or habits, which have been wrought into our nature and remain permanently with us, and which are called into consciousness by present surroundings. In the former case, the course of conduct is literally the creature of present surroundings; in the latter, however, present surroundings have but little to do in determining the course of conduct.

49. *The child's course of conduct in after-life, his character and moral strength, depend very largely upon the method of control adopted by his parents and teachers during infancy and childhood.*

(*a*). This proposition necessarily follows from the position stated in 48 (*b*). The boy who has been controlled by present enjoyments, supplied by an indulgent parent or teacher, becomes strangely changed in his conduct when he passes into less favorable surroundings. The amiable and well-behaved boy in the mother's sitting-room or in the teacher's class-room, becomes all at once unreliable and vicious. This is almost the invariable product of that method of governing children which controls them by simply supplying present gratification.

(*b*). The position stated in 48 (*b*) points to another method of control. Present enjoyment should not be ignored, yet it should be made simply a means to an end. While ministering to the child's enjoyment, it is the imperative duty of both parent and teacher to see that true principles of action and correct habits are wrought into his being. These he will carry with him as a permanent possession, and they will determine his course of conduct when he ceases to be under the influence of pleasant surroundings supplied by the kind hand of another.

PERIOD OF YOUTH.

This period commences between the ages of twelve and sixteen, and ends between the ages of twenty and twenty-five. The chief points which demand the special attention of parents and teachers are set forth in the following propositions:

50. *The body at the beginning of this period is in a transition state, and demands special attention in order to prevent mistakes which may result in permanent injury.*

(*a*). New experiences growing out of physical changes make their appearance at the beginning of this period. These experiences in their nature are ex-

citing and taxing upon the nervous energies. They
are also accompanied by a strong natural tendency to
sacrifice largely the other vital interests of the body
in order that they may be enjoyed. Hence, at this
particular stage of development, there is great danger
of fatal injury to the body growing out of the viola-
tion of simple physiological laws.

(*b*). A large share of the ruinous practices which
prevail during this period is the result of ignorance of
the fatal consequences accompanying these practices
and of the proper treatment of the body. It is,
therefore, the imperative duty of parents, and in case
they fail to do the work, then of teachers, to give, at
the proper time and under proper restrictions, such instructions as will make plain the evils to be avoided,
and as will impart strength and determination to avoid
them. Recourse in this matter should be had to the
instructions given upon the subject in standard authorities on physiology and hygiene.

(*c*). All concede that the condition of the body affects
directly the experiences of the mind. When a man is
"blue," it is usually safe to conclude that his digestive
organs are somewhat out of order. It is no more true
that the body affects the mind than that the conditions
and states of the mind affect the body. The feelings
and passions react upon the body and induce courses
of conduct which bring upon it disease and ruin.
Here it should be carefully noted that physical debility
or disease as a reaction from the mind is the result of
passive, not active, states of mind—is the result of an

over-exercise of the feelings, the emotions, the passions, and not of the intellect, the reason, the judgment. By keeping the feelings and the emotions nearly inactive, a boy or girl between the ages of fifteen and twenty-five can perform, without the slightest injury to the body, far more of what may be called purely intellectual work than is now usually performed in any of our schools.

51. *During this period all the products of the intellectual nature, including the reasoning power, judgment, etc., carry with them the authority of intuitions.*

(*a*). Sense-products absorb largely the attention during infancy and childhood. Accompanying this condition of things, a gradual transformation is going on. The mind is becoming more and more interested in simple inferences that follow readily from the sense-perceptions acquired. As a result, at the beginning of the third period simple processes of reasoning, such as each mind is prepared for, become more intensely absorbing than even sense-products. Facts already acquired are now assuming a new interest, and are again looked over and compared, and conclusions reached which were no part of the original perceptions. These conclusions are simple and direct, and hence are necessarily as real to the mind as the propositions themselves. Consequently they carry with them the same positive authority as the perceptions.

(*b*). As a necessary consequence of the transformation named in (*a*), a marked characteristic of youth i ; developed; namely, the habit of drawing conclusions from insufficient premises. This habit is the natural result of the direct method of making inferences practised in infancy and childhood. So strong does it become before commencing a course of training where rigid demonstrations are required, that the mind refuses to recognize as necessary the series of steps on which a conclusion is based. The conclusion is perceived, and in a certain sense as a conclusion, without taking into account in logical order the premises on which it rests. This condition of things is the reason why so many bright children, possessed of marked perceptive powers, strongly dislike the demonstrative sciences. If, however, such children are properly guided by their teachers, they will very soon become intensely interested in the examination of data and premises for the purpose of determining whether the conclusions drawn are legitimate and in accordance with the truth of things.

(*c*). Other very important characteristics of youth have their origin in the condition of things stated in the above proposition. For example, boys and girls during this period are naturally skeptical, conceited, and positive even to obstinacy. They think they know things just as they are, and that there is little to be known outside of what they have examined. This is a legitimate consequence of the peeuliarly new and authoritative nature of their present intellectual products. The child's perceptions of the objective world are intensely real to him. He entertains no doubts regarding them. He looks with astonishment at any one who would call in question these perceptions. In this peculiar sense the child may be said to be very skeptical. In this third period a similar condition of things prevails regarding the perceptions of the reasoning powers. These perceptions are also new and authoritative, and contain to the young mind just about the whole truth. Hence, as in the case of the child, grave doubts, which assume frequently the form of conceit and obstinacy, are entertained of anything that seems to contradict this authoritative experience. Young men and young women in this good sense are skeptical, conceited, and even obstinate; but this skepticism, conceit, and obstinacy, properly directed and controlled by competent teachers, become most desirable qualities in building a strong and vigorous manhood and womanhood.

52. *The social nature at the beginning of this period commences to assert control, and hence demands the special attention of parents and teachers.*

(*a*). During infancy and childhood the element of sex has played but a small part in the social intercourse of boys and girls. They have thus far associated together in sports and common enjoyments. They have formed attachments growing out of these associations. Now, however, another and more subtle element than sports and common enjoyments determines the attachments formed. Now to the boy the society of girls is becoming more attractive than that of boys, and to the girl the society of boys than that of girls. This condition of things is in the order of nature. The evident duty, therefore, of parents and teachers is to direct and control, not to crush, this inherent and refining natural tendency of our being.

(*b*). The emotional nature and the imagination play a very important part in shaping the social relations and the general course of conduct of this period. It is a common saying—"boys and girls are impulsive." We mean by this that they act from their feelings rather than from the dictates of their reason and judgment. In this connection it should be carefully noted that the emotional nature is exceedingly inventive, and that this inventive power is in some degree universal. There are comparatively few, who, in matters requiring the exercise of pure intellect, are inventive; yet every one, in matters pertaining to the feelings, possesses this power. This is particularly true between the ages of fifteen and twenty-five. Hence the endless variety of devices by which young people are able to carry out the demands of the feelings and of the heart; hence, also, the importance of supplying the proper social conditions for the exercise and training of this power.

(*c*). An over-exercise of the social nature, which draws so largely upon the feelings or emotions, is productive of great injury both to the body and to the mind. The effect of such a course upon the body has already been pointed out in 50 (*c*). A similar effect is produced upon the mind by such a course. Rugged and clear thinking, even in the case of what may be called strong and matured minds, soon becomes impossible if the emotional nature is overtaxed. The intellectual vigor of boys and girls is not unfrequently undermined by indulgences in social life and by the reading of sensational books, both of which make a strong draft upon the feelings. Under such conditions they soon reach a point where they spend a large share of their time in a dreamy passive state. They lose all desire for positive, active, vigorous mental work. This is only one of the many evil results of over-indulgence of the social nature, so commonly permitted and even encouraged by parents of the present time. There is a golden mean in this matter, and parents and teachers should not fail to adopt it, as either extreme is productive of great injury.

53. *The development and training of the moral nature should receive the first attention of parents and teachers during each of these three periods. Under proper guidance all the activities of the intellectual nature may gradually be subordinated, as they ought to be, to the control of the conscience and will.*

(*a*). The conscience is as susceptible of education as any other power of the mind. Its development runs parallel with the development of the intellectual powers. It manifests itself in infancy in enforcing obedience to the simple laws of nature learned through experience. The *ought to be* and *ought not to be* enters very early into the child's consciousness. Indeed, it accompanies every experience he passes through where he knows that one of two courses would avoid pain or suffering. A mistake is very commonly made regarding the province of the conscience. It is practically restricted by many in its operations to what is known as the spiritual part of our being. Conscience to such has nothing to do with the ordinary exercise of the functions of the body. This is a great mistake, and leads to fatal results in the training of the infant and child. The decisions of the conscience are coextensive with the work of our entire being. They alone settle authoritatively *when, where, how* and *for what purpose* each function of the body and each power of the mind *ought* to be exercised.

(*b*). The development and training of the conscience is usually sadly neglected. From infancy up to manhood, in all matters pertaining to the intellect, every encouragement is given to independent action, and the results and decisions reached are respected. It is assumed in this case that there is an inherent power in the child to see things as they are that can be trusted. And because of this assumption, such work and exercises are intrusted to the child as develop and train his intellectual powers in a proper manner. The opposite of this course is pursued with the conscience. From infancy up, the child is treated as if he had no *spiritual eye*, by which to see the *ought to be* and the *ought not to be*. His parents and his teacher's spiritual eyes are supposed to do all the seeing where the " ought to be " and the " ought not to be " are to be considered. He is expected, simply, machine like, to execute orders without any regard even to the existence of his conscience. Such a course, and it is a very common one, soon dwarfs and warps the conscience so that its authority is little felt or regarded.

(*c*). The proper development of the moral nature demands that the conscience should be constantly called into exercise. Commencing with infancy, the child should be guided so that he will acquire the habit of considering always before doing a thing, whether it *ought* or *ought not* to be done. This habit should not, as is frequently the case, have reference to one or two classes of acts, as, for example, obedience to parents, and truthfulness. It should be co-extensive with the child's activities, including the exercises of the body and of the mind. Here it should be carefully noted, that the decisions of the child's conscience have reference to the child's view of the conditions presented. They should be judged and respected as such. The development of the moral nature is possible only by requiring the child to exercise his conscience in making decisions for himself regarding the " ought to be " and the " ought not to be," and to act upon these decisions when made. This course should be pursued from infancy to manhood by both parents and teachers. In all kinds of school work, as well as in matters of conduct, there should be a systematic, constant, and direct exercise of the conscience. Pupils should not be forced or induced to perform their work, or to pursue a required course of conduct simply by the use of artificial devices, such as marks, prizes, and so forth. These devices may be used so as to secure present results, but they never leave a permanent impression upon the mind which will be of service in their absence in controlling and directing both work and conduct.

PRINCIPLES OF PUPIL'S WORK.

Under this head will be outlined the principles which concern the work that should be performed by pupils during their educational course. No attempt is made, however, to outline the special studies or exercises that should be pursued. The suggestions given are of a general nature and will apply to the execution of any curriculum that may be adopted.

54. *The work performed by pupils should accomplish two general results; namely, self-development and self-equipment.*

(*a*). The word *work* in this proposition is used in a broad sense. It includes every line of self-activity which has for its object the legitimate development and equipment of body and of mind, as well as what is generally known as work proper, or productive effort. Rightly directed sports, calisthenics, gymnastics, etc., are as truly a part of the work which should be required of pupils as the study of books. The truth of this position is now fully recognized in the kindergarten, but its application is no more important there than at every stage of the pupil's progress until graduating from college. Hence it is as imperative a duty to supply the conditions that will *rightly direct* the pupil's physical exercises and amusements, throughout his entire educational course, as it is to apply the conditions that will *rightly direct* his efforts in acquiring knowledge. l

(*b*). Self-development is of two kinds; namely, *general* and *special* or *professional*. The nature and extent of the former has already been outlined (Arts. 8 to 40 inclusive). The latter has reference to the peculiar development or training which fits a person for a special work. The training, for example, which fits a physician to make a correct diagnosis, or an accountant to make accurate and rapid calculations, is of this kind. Special development or training should invariably follow and be based upon a thorough course of general training, and should be the result of lines of work arranged specially for that purpose.

(*c*). Self-equipment is also of two kinds; namely, *general* and *special* or *professional*. The former has reference to the acquisition of such power, aptitudes, methods of work, and knowledge of materials and appliances as will give a thorough general preparation for any calling in life. The latter has reference to the acquisition of such additional professional preparation as may be necessary for effective service in a special calling. This should be invariably based upon, and should follow the former as an easy and natural consequence. It should simply be the result of supplementing the power, aptitudes and methods of work already acquired by such new knowledge of materials and appliances as belong specially to the chosen calling. This should be accomplished by pursuing lines of work arranged with special reference to that end.

(*d*). Self-equipment, when completed, should include, in addition to what has been noted in (*c*), the acquisition upon the part of pupils of the following : (1) A definite knowledge of the resources within themselves, as well as those outside of themselves, upon which they can constantly draw for personal enjoyment and for intellectual, moral and spiritual growth ; (2) Habits and tastes for reading standard authors in History, Biography, Literature, Science, etc., which will insure the constant companionship of the choicest spirits of all ages, and prove an effectual bar against indulging in lines of pleasure and reading which are destructive of manly and womanly growth ; (3) Such knowledge of human nature, and such sympathy with all classes and conditions of persons, as will fit them to enter into right and effective co-operative relations in business, in social life, and in beneficent efforts to render help to those who are in need of it. If the educational work of pupils does not secure to them these three things, in addition to what has been referred to in notes (*b*) and (*c*), it must be regarded as largely a failure.

55. Self-activity is the fundamental condition of all healthy development, both of the body and of the mind.

(*a*). Self-activity is of two kinds; namely, spontaneous and voluntary. This distinction is one of great importance to the true educator. It indicates clearly the only two classes of activity by which the development and equipment of the body and of the mind are directly accomplished. It marks, therefore, sharply the central elements in the pupil's nature to which teachers must direct their attention and effort in the execution of their work.

(*b*). Spontaneous self-activity in the case of the body includes, for example, such activity as is involved in the various processes of nutrition by which physical growth and repair are carried on. This form of self-activity is, however, only one of two elements in physical development. The other element is voluntary self-activity, which takes the form of sports, work, and physical exercise of various sorts. These two elements are inseparably joined to each other in the process of physical development. Their co-operation, under right conditions and in right proportions, is the chief means by which a vigorous and healthy body is produced. Here it should be noted that, of these two elements, spontaneous self-activity stands first, and its exercise determines the limits of voluntary self-activity. When the functions of nutrition, for example, are weak, either naturally or from obstructing causes, physical exercise, either in the form of sports or work, must be carefully guarded in order to protect the body from permanent injury.

(*c*). The relation of spontaneous to voluntary self-activity in the case of the body, pointed out in (*b*), holds equally true in regard to the mind. Here spontaneous self-activity includes, for example, the unconscious mental process by which truth is digested and assimilated as stated in Art. 40 (*b*). This unconscious mental process performs the same function in the development of mind that nutrition does in the development of the body. The voluntary self-activity of the mind also includes the processes of observing, comparing, willing, etc. These processes correspond in the development of mind to physical exercises of various kinds in the development of the body.

(*d*). From what has just been stated in notes (*b*) and (*c*), it will be seen that the success of our efforts for the development and equipment of the body and of the mind depends upon the vigorous and rightly-adjusted exercise of spontaneous and voluntary self-activity. This fact is now generally recognized and acted upon in reference to the body. In this case, the condition of the process of nutrition regulates the kind and degree of physical effort that will best promote a healthy physical growth. The fixed and dependent relation of these two kinds of activity is, as already pointed out, as true of the mind as of the body. Hence the condition of the unconscious process of mental digestion and assimilation regulates the kind and degree of voluntary mental effort which will best promote a healthy mental development. Teachers failing to recognize and act upon this important fact, have frequently inflicted permanent mental injury upon their pupils by forcing them to undertake mental work which requires the exercise of voluntary mental activity far beyond what is warranted by their mental ability to digest and assimilate truth.

56. *Work, rightly adapted to the needs of the pupils, is the principal means to be used to secure their self-development and self-equipment.*

(*a*). Work in this proposition includes every line of self-activity which contributes legitimately, and without waste of time or energy, to the self-development and self-equipment of the pupils. Much of the work now performed in schools fails of this result. Pupils are frequently forced to waste their time and energy in a fruitless effort to do work which is entirely beyond their present power of self-activity.

(*b*). *The work must be exactly suited to the capacity of the pupils.* This means that the work assigned at any time must be such as can be performed by the pupils themselves, by a proper exercise of the self-activity they possess at that time. This condition is violated almost universally in regard to some lines of work required in schools and colleges. Pupils are constantly confronted with work for which their power of self-activity is entirely inadequate. The only course left in such cases is to leave the work undone, or to have the pupils carried through it by injurious helps rendered by teachers. The former is decidedly the better course of the two, but either results in permanent injury to the pupils.

(c). The work must be such as will accomplish in the act of performing it the ends for which it is to be performed. There should be a definite end accomplished by every kind of work assigned to pupils. This end may not always be apparent to the pupils, but the teacher must, in every case, have a clear conception of it in order to be able rightly to guide the pupils in their work. Here it must be carefully noted that the ends to be accomplished must always determine the kind of work that should be assigned and the method of doing it. Hence, teachers must clearly apprehend these ends in order rightly to assign work, as well as to guide in its performance. Failing in this respect, they will of necessity waste their own time as well as the time and energy of their pupils in aimless and injurious efforts. The pupils in this case will be kept busy in doing a little of everything and nothing, in *doing* and *undoing*, in going through the forms of work, while practically accomplishing nothing of real value. Much of the work done in many schools, in the lower branches, is of this kind. A large share of the time and effort spent upon reading, arithmetic, grammar, geography, composition and like subjects is actually worse than wasted, because of its aimless character. The illegitimate use frequently made of memory, in each of these lines of work, illustrates this waste. Pupils, for example, are required to fix in their memory definitions, rules, forms of analysis, and other details which to them, at the time, are meaningless, and which, after being recited, must necessarily be very

soon forgotten. All work of this kind is very largely a waste of time and energy and fails to accomplish the end for which it is performed.

Again, the method in which pupils are required to perform their work must be guarded with as much care as the kind of work assigned them. The importance of this is well illustrated in the study of languages. A language is usually studied for one of two purposes: first, to use as an instrument for oral or written communication with others, or second, to use as an exegetical instrument. In acquiring a language for either of these purposes some of the work should be performed exactly in the same way. It is, however, a great mistake to insist, as some do, that the same method should be pursued in performing the entire work. The critical study, for example, of the technicalities of grammar and of fine lexical distinctions, however extensively and thoroughly pursued, will never give to the student the power of speaking a language correctly or even of writing it with ease and correctness. If this is the end sought, such work is not necessary, and hence, if performed, is a waste of the pupil's time. On the other hand, this is the very work that must be thoroughly done if the end sought is to become a reliable exegete. The importance of adapting a method of doing the work to the end to be accomplished is quite as marked in the study of some other subjects as in languages. Hence the care that should be taken by teachers to master thoroughly, in every subject, the relation between method and end.

(*d*). *The arrangement of the work must harmonize with the order of self-development.* This course must be pursued during the formative period of the educational process. But as the pupils advance and become independent workers, the logical order of the subjects studied should be regarded, and finally should control in the arrangement of work assigned. Until independence is possible, however, the controlling principle in determining the nature and arrangement of the work should be the order of self-development. This order can be ascertained and properly understood only as the result of a careful study of the physical and psychical forces by which development is produced at every stage of the entire formative period. The ascertained action of these forces indicates that the arrangement of work should conform substantially with the following:

(1). The amount of self-activity a pupil can put forth in one act must always determine how difficult each *step* of *work* assigned should be made. In reference to this statement, it should be observed that by a *step* of *work* is meant the amount of work a pupil should be required to undertake in one effort or act. This may be called the pupil's unit of work. What this unit should be in every case must be determined by the teacher, and should be gradually increased as the pupil's power of self-activity increases. Each step or unit of work assigned should be made sufficiently difficult to entice effort, but not so difficult as either to strain or to discourage. Pupils like to do difficult things when presented to them in a way to afford pleasure and hence incite action.

(2). The work must be arranged step by step, so that each *step* or *unit* can be performed by pupils by the exercise of their own self-activity. Teachers should aid or supplement the self-activity of their pupils, first, by the way in which they place the work before them, second, by supplying right incentives to action, and third, by guarding them against wrongly applying their strength in doing the work. Usually, when such aid as this fails, the work should be left un-done until the self-development of the pupils makes them equal to the task. It is no part of the duty of teachers to do the work of their pupils, or by the use of false helps to carry their pupils blindly over work for which their present power of self-activity is unequal. Teachers who make such a work their duty do a great injury to their pupils.

(3). The arrangement of the work must be such that each step, when performed, will prepare the pupils properly for the next step in advance. Each advanced step should follow easily and naturally from the pre-ceding step.

57. The work of pupils should be of such a nature and should be conducted in such a way as to give to them a thorough mastery of fundamental principles, while avoiding entirely waste of time and effort upon uncalled-for details.

(*a*). A large share of the time and energy of the

pupils is spent in many schools upon the acquisition of details, which, in the very nature of things, will be acquired without effort when the right time comes. Many of these details stand related to the growth of root-principles of the mind, in the same way as leaves stand related to the growth of the roots and stem of a plant. The leaves will come of themselves when the necessary growth of root and stem takes place. In like manner these details will come of themselves when the necessary growth of the root-principles of the mind on which they depend has taken place. It would certainly be regarded as a very foolish waste of time and effort to attempt by artificial processes to put leaves upon plants. It is no less foolish a waste of time and effort to attempt by artificial means to fix in the memory of pupils, at the wrong time, details which will, at the right time, take their place there as the necessary products of mind growth, as naturally as the leaves take their place upon plants as the necessary products of plant growth.

(*b*). The reason generally assigned for the time and effort spent in acquiring these artificial and uncalled-for details is the mental discipline which the exercise affords. This reason is certainly not based upon a good foundation. But even granting that some mental discipline is acquired, the same mental discipline can be had in much larger measure by performing work whose products are not to pass out of the mind as soon as the recitation is over; work which will also supply material for constant mental activity, and which will broaden the field of the pupil's knowledge. Aside, however, from any other consideration, the fundamentals of mental growth and of knowledge are too many and too important to allow a single day of the pupil's time to be spent upon acquiring details which serve scarcely any purpose, and which necessarily pass out of mind in a short time.

(*c*). But, again, the artificial acquisition of uncalled-for details so commonly practiced in our schools does a greater injury to pupils than to waste their time and effort. It substitutes artificial and unrelated material for the mental aliment necessary for real mind growth. And hence it actually starves mentally a large number of the very brightest pupils. Such pupils usually become soured and disgusted with school work simply because of the meaningless drudgery they are required to perform in fixing in the memory useless details. In short, this entire course makes impossible, in a very large degree, the exercise of that kind of self-activity by which alone the physical and mental development and equipment of the pupils can be accomplished.

58. The work of pupils from the infant class on through college should be conducted in such a manner as to cause them to acquire a systematic method of doing every thing they undertake.

(*a*). Pupils, in performing their work, should invariably follow the course of an investigator and not that of an original discoverer. The latter is in search of the unknown, not only to himself but to all else besides; hence every step taken is involved in a degree of uncertainty. Hypothesis after hypothesis may have to be made and rejected before reaching a final result. This process is necessarily slow, and it is also the work of a mind already trained rather than that of one needing training. Pupils are not in any case original discoverers in this sense. They are in search of what is to them unknown but what is fully and clearly known to others. This distinction places the work of pupils upon an entirely different basis from that of an original discoverer. In all their investigations and search after truth they should therefore be guided by their teachers in taking advantage of methods, means and material already discovered and in successful use by investigators of recognized standing. None of their time should be wasted in going through the slow and necessarily uncertain steps of the original discoverer. The field of work they should undertake is too extensive to admit of such a course.

(*b*). What is commonly known as the *Inductive Method* is the true course to pursue in all rightly conducted educational work. This statement, however, if understood in an unlimited sense, includes too much. In the educational process, when rightly carried on, *Induction* and *Deduction* must go hand in hand. The former always precedes the latter, but both are equally necessary as means of mental development and instruments of work. Pupils, therefore, fail of right mental development and of right equipment who are not able to perform work successfully in which each of these methods must necessarily be used.

(*c*). **The** Inductive Method of investigation or of performing mental work consists of four steps; namely, Observation, Comparison and Classification, Deduction, Verification. Before stating the nature and application of each of these steps, it is necessary to note that Observation includes three forms of mental activity; namely, Sensation, Sense Perception and Ideation. Sensation denotes the mental activity called feeling, which is produced by impressions made on the sensitive organs; Sense Perception denotes the mental activity which cognizes an outward object as the cause of feeling; and Ideation denotes the mental activity which forms a definite representation or idea in the mind of the object of Sense Perception. A treatise on psychology must be consulted for a full statement of the nature and relation of these three forms of mental activity to each other and their place in the educational process. It must, however, be stated here that the acquisition upon the part of pupils of an acute sensitiveness to impressions made upon the organs of sense, and also of strong and active powers of sense perception and of ideation, is a matter of vital importance to their progress in mental growth and in mental work.

(*d*). Observation, the first step in the Inductive Method, consists of a systematic search for existing facts, for what is, and an examination of the nature of these facts and their relation to each other This search and examination is, in the first place, confined to noting the structure and nature of individual objects or definite units of investigation, and is usually conducted in one of four ways: First, the work may be performed by the use of the senses alone; second, by the use of the senses supplemented by instruments such as the eyeglass, microscope, telescope, etc.; third, by the use of the senses supplemented by experiments in which apparatus and various mechanical devices are used, as in chemistry, physics, etc.; fourth, by the use of the senses, without what is known as apparatus, but supplemented by experiments, in which various kinds of changes are made in the object under examination, in its form, conditions of existence, representation, etc., such as are of service in the study of Reading, Languages, Mathematics, Botany, Physiology, etc.

(*e*). In conducting Observation, the object or unit of investigation must first be viewed as a whole. Then, step by step, each fact in reference to the structure and nature of the object is noted, until the vague whole of the first act is seen to consist of an aggregate of parts possessing various properties. Thus it will be seen that *Observation* is, in a certain sense, an analytic or decomposing process by which the mind is placed in conscious relations to all of the elements which constitute a given complex unit or whole. This process, rightly conducted, involves three steps. In the first step a note is made of all the facts as they exist or of what is, and in the second of the relation existing between these parts or between the elements composing the unit under consideration.   After these two steps, which are usually regarded as Observation proper, have been completed, a third step, of a differ-ent nature, must be taken in order to give pupils the full mental benefit of the work performed.   The third step consists of a synthetic mental effort by which all the facts, elements and relations noted are formed into a mental unit or idea representing the object ob-served, and to which a name is attached by which it can be recalled at pleasure and made the subject of thought, in the absence of the object which it repre-sents.   This last step is one of vital importance in men-tal development.   The other two steps fill an import-ant place, but they may be performed with apparent success without resulting in any valuable mental strength.   Indeed, where the third step is partially or wholly neglected, they result in weakening rather than in strengthening mental effort.   Pupils, in such a case, gradually become helplessly dependent for mental activity upon the actual presence of the objects. Such a result is to be carefully avoided, but this can only be done by persistently making each pupil complete the process of observation by forming a vivid mental pict-ure of the object observed in the way indicated in the third step.

(*f*). The process of Observation, including Ideation or the third step referred to in (*c*), is fundamental to every kind of work which must be performed by pu-pils in the act of developing and equipping their minds. It is the key to the highest success at every stage of the pupil's progress in the study of languages, mathematics, physical and mental sciences, theology, philosophy and every other department of mental effort. Hence the importance of rightly initiating and directing pupils in acquiring the power and forming the habit of performing every line of their work in this way cannot be overestimated or too strongly emphasized. The training in this matter should commence in the infant class and should be continued throughout the entire educational course. During the earlier stages of school life the observations of pupils cannot be used as reliable data on which to base conclusions. This condition of things will, however, gradually disappear if teachers give proper and earnest attention to the training of the senses, and guide their pupils in their use in each of the four ways pointed out in (*d*). Here it should be noted that only observations conducted by trained senses, under the guidance and control of a trained intellect and will, can supply reliable data on which to base conclusions that are final. Hence the care that must be taken in guiding pupils in observing and collecting data from which they are required to deduce principles, laws, formulas, rules, or definitions.

(*g*). Comparison and Classification, the second step in the Inductive Method, consists of the process by which general propositions are formed from observed particulars. This process is in fact a farther application of Observation, including Ideation, or the third step referred to in (*e*) Observation proper, as considered in (*d*), is restricted to noting the facts in reference to the nature and structure of individual objects or definite units of investigation of any kind. When this work is exhaustively performed, and the facts observed in reference to each of a number of objects have been arranged in groups by themselves, the work of Observation proper is completed and the material is ready for *Comparison* and *Classification*. This step consists in comparing the groups of elements or properties formed by Observation, and noting, first, how many of these elements or properties are possessed in common by all of the objects, and second, that the elements or properties possessed in common can be affirmed equally of each of the objects, and hence that a general proposition can be formed making this affirmation. It should here be carefully observed that general propositions formed in this way are general only in the sense that the predicate applies to all of the objects, represented by the subject of the proposition, which have been included in the previous process of Observation.

(*h*). In reference to the nature of Deduction, the third step in the Inductive Method, and the grounds on which the process is based there are different views held by good authorities. As to the relative merits of these views, works on Inductive Logic must be consulted. In this connection, however, the subject must be regarded simply as an element of the educational process; as such the practical and perhaps commonly accepted view is all that need be stated. From this standpoint, therefore, *Deduction*, as the third step in the Inductive Method, may be defined as the process by which we determine when the predicate of a general proposition can be affirmed of an object which was not included among the objects observed when the proposition was originally formed. The practical application of this process is very varied. The correctness of the conclusion reached in any given case depends largely upon the intuitive acuteness of the observer, and upon the closeness of the relation of the nature and structure of the object presented to the objects considered in forming the original proposition. Suppose, for example, the general proposition to be, Oxen *chew the cud*, and that this was formed from observations made upon ten specimens. In case another ox is presented differing in size, color and general appearance from those examined, the conclusion would be readily drawn that he also *chews the cud*. This conclusion would be based not upon identity but upon marked resemblance in structure. But now suppose a bison in place of another ox is presented, the conclusion would not be so readily drawn, if at all, and still less so if a deer is substituted for the bison. Yet in both of these cases a more careful observation of resemblances in structure and habits would undoubtedly lead to the conclusion that both chew the cud. Deductions of this sort are never to be regarded as absolutely certain until verified. They possess, however, varied degrees of certainty, according to the conditions under which they are made. This fact must be impressed upon pupils, and they must be carefully trained in recognizing readily data from which reliable deductions can be made. This is important, as the process of *Deduction*, or third step of the inductive method, is the chief means through which their knowledge, in every line of investigation, is systematically broadened.

(*i*). Verification, the fourth step in the Inductive Method, consists in the process of verifying deductions made by means of the third step as outlined in note (*h*). This is done by submitting the object or unit in reference to which the deduction is made to the same scrutiny by Observation and by Comparison and Classification as was given the objects with which it is, by Deduction, now classified. The notes on Observation and on Comparison and Classification can be referred to in regard to the manner of conducting the process of *Verification*.

PRINCIPLES OF TEACHERS' WORK.

There are at least a few general principles which all teachers should regard in performing their work. These, however, are of such a nature as to leave teachers perfectly free to exercise, in every respect, their own individuality. The work of teachers, like all other kinds of work, can be conducted successfully only by men and women who bring to it a strong personality; a personality which will assert itself in original methods of doing things suited to the special conditions under which the work must be performed. Persons of this sort are usually possessed of tact and a good degree of common sense, and hence, while working in their own "harness," will take advantage of, and be guided by, principles that have given success to others in doing a similar line of work. Such persons among teachers are always ready and anxious to study and apply all suggestions coming from the experience of others. Hence the following outline of principles is not given with the view of setting forth a fixed method of teaching which all should blindly follow, but rather for the purpose of presenting materials and suggestions which may be helpful to teachers as a basis for careful thought upon the way in which their work should be conducted.

GENERAL PRINCIPLES.

59. *The work of teachers is co-extensive with the entire educational process by which both the body and the mind of their pupils are developed and equipped.*

(*a*). The view, very commonly entertained, which regards teachers simply as *instructors* or the *mediums* through which the pupils are to *acquire knowledge* is entirely wrong. This is ouly a very small part of their work. Their work includes a much more important and wider range than this. It has to do not only with imparting knowledge, but with every line of physical and mental activity which contributes in any way to developing and equipping their pupils.

It has, therefore, to do with molding every phase of the nature of the pupils, including the physical, intellectual, moral and spiritual. Hence the way in which this work is understood and performed will determine the nature and extent of the products of the educational course of the pupils.

(*b*). The nature and extent of the work to be performed determines the qualifications which teachers should possess. These qualifications should be such as will place them in vital and helpful relation to their pupils in every line of effort their pupils must pursue in promoting self-development and self-equipment.

60. *The work of teachers in a general sense consists in supplying the conditions or occasions for the vigorous and healthful exercise of the self-activities of their pupils.*

(*a*). Teachers are, in an important sense, co-workers with their pupils, but this does not mean that they are to join with their pupils and actually perform a part of their work. They are co-workers not in this sense, but in the sense of conditioning their pupils so that they can and will of themselves perform the work assigned to them. On the carefulness with which teachers pursue this course will depend the amount of real good they will render their pupils in the matter of self-development and preparation for becoming effective workers in their life calling. The following hints in reference to this course and in reference to what teachers cannot do for their pupils should be noted.

(*b*). Teachers, in conditioning properly their pupils for their work, should see that their surroundings are made pleasant, that they are supplied with plenty of fresh and healthful air, that they are kept entirely free from petty annoyances from fellow pupils, and from needless requirements and restrictions, that their time for doing their work is systematically arranged and that right physical exercises are provided at proper intervals during the school hours. All these conditions are properly within the control of energetic and rightly qualified teachers, and should receive special attention because they are of real importance to the success of their pupils in their work.

(*c*). Teachers, in rightly conditioning their pupils, must supply them with proper incentives in their work. These incentives must be varied according to the age, advancement in study, past and present environments, special ambitions, and other conditions peculiar to the pupils. But in no case should false incentives be used which have only a present and perhaps momentary effect, such as sweetmeats, promises of certain selfish indulgences, gifts and prizes. Incentives of the right kind should invariably have their origin in the kind of work performed, in the manner of performing it, in the knowledge or other products to be attained, in the ideal end of every effort in the way of self-development, and in present pleasant experiences as the result of successful effort. These incentives must be constantly held before the pupils in the life of their teachers, both in word and deed, in precept and example. Teachers should be an inspiration to their pupils in all these things. Their own earnest, prompt and systematic performance of every work should be one of the strongest incentives to their pupils to pursue a like course. Their watchword in every line of effort should always be *come* and not *go*.

(*d*). Teachers, in rightly conditioning their pupils for their work, must see that the work assigned is properly adapted to the present power of self-activity possessed by the pupils (Art. 56) (*b*), that it is rightly arranged so that every step prepares for the next (Art. 56) (*d*), that it is rightly executed, and that the final products are reduced to systematized knowledge.. In this matter everything depends upon the qualifications of the teachers for their work. They will fail in supplying these conditions unless they have definite and clear views regarding them and are possessed of the power that will enable them rightly to execute their views.

(*e*). Teachers, in seeking to condition their pupils properly for their work, must note carefully what they cannot do for them. No person, for example, can digest or assimilate food for another, nor take for another the exercise and rest necessary for this purpose. In this case the only help one person can render another is to supply healthful food in proper quantities and at proper times, and also right conditions for needed exercise and rest. What is true of the development of the body is equally true of the development of the mind. No person can perceive, feel, reason, or understand for another. All operations of the mind, by which it is developed, are as strictly personal as the functions of nutrition in reference to the body. Each mind must do its own work or else it remains forever undone. We can acquire experiences of all sorts, but we cannot impart them to any one else. All we can do in this case for others is to supply them with the conditions through which our experiences came to us. The mental effort put forth by us in gaining these experiences must be put forth by every one else who would acquire precisely the same experiences and the mental development accompanying them. This is true not only of intellectual, but also of moral and spiritual experiences.

61. *Teachers should possess substantially the following general qualifications in order to be able rightly to condition their pupils for the development of a reliable and symmetrical character.*

(*a*). They should possess a reliable, transparent and unimpeachable character and a strong personality, marked by tact and good common sense.

(*b*). They should possess the power of forming, intuitively, a reliable estimate of the real character of their pupils, and of the forces by which their conduct is directed and controlled.

(*c*). They should possess a commanding presence, accompanied by a sympathetic nature, guided by a sensitive conscience and firm and controlling will.

(*d*). They should be true to every duty and personal conviction, yet generous and fair in their treatment of the convictions of others, recognizing in the fullest sense the principle of "*Soul Liberty*," and maintaining in acts, as well as in words, the "*Golden Rule*" as the true standard of life's conduct.

(*e*). They should be sympathetic towards their pupils, giving to them their confidence and rendering them effective help whenever necessary.

(*f*). They should be entirely impartial in all their dealings with their pupils. Their course in this respect should be so transparent that no pupil can fail to recognize the just and unbiased character of their actions.

(*g*). They should exercise a kind and diligent watchfulness over every step in the progress of their pupils in manly and womanly self-development, surrounding them constantly with the most favorable conditions to promote this end.

(*h*). They should be models to their pupils in all things that pertain to personal conduct, or that pertain to any line of school work in which pupils are engaged. They should never fail to sustain by their own acts every requirement they make of their pupils.

The foregoing general qualifications are fundamental, as they constitute the basis which gives effectiveness to all others. Teachers who are defective in these, however well qualified for their work in other respects, must of necessity largely fail in rightly conditioning their pupils for the successful development of a trustworthy character.

SPECIAL PRINCIPLES OF TEACHING.

Under this head are outlined the principles of mental activity which should invariably guide teachers in the work of imparting instruction. Teaching proper is the process by which teachers condition the minds of their pupils so that they may be able: (*a*) To gain a clear, accurate and comprehensive knowledge of all the truths involved in each subject on which they receive instruction; (*b*) To digest and assimilate the truths acquired and make them a permanent possession, which can be recalled to consciousness whenever occasion requires; (*c*) To discover the practical applications of the knowledge acquired in the common affairs of life, and to gain the ability to make these applications. When teachers condition their pupils so as to accomplish successfully each of these three ends they will, at the same time, condition them so as to accomplish in the best manner their self-development and self-equipment. The following propositions and notes suggest the way in which this work should be done.

62. *The mind must gain through the senses its knowledge of everything external to itself*

(*a*). This proposition is self-evident and should be the invariable guide of teachers in conditioning their pupils in gaining a knowledge of material things.

(*b*). In every case possible, when an object is first studied it should be present to the senses. But as soon as clearly defined in the mind it should be withdrawn, and pupils should be required by the exercise of Ideation to continue the object before the mind as a definite subject of thought. The continuance of the use of objects beyond the limit stated is a source of weakness and permanent injury to the pupils.

(*c*). When the objects studied cannot be present to the sense, as in geography and similar subjects, models should be used, and, where this cannot be done, drawings and pictures. It must here be noted, however, that subjects of this kind can only be studied properly after pupils have acquired sufficient power in the exercise of constructive imagination to enable them, by the aid of a model, drawing or picture to construct a correct and vivid representation in their own minds of the real objects they are engaged in studying. It must not be forgotten that, until this power is acquired, models, drawings and pictures are to the pupils just what they appear to be to their senses, hence they fail almost entirely to comprehend the true nature of the objects on which instruction is attempted to be given.

(*d*). In the use of objects three ends are to be accomplished. *First*, the power of the senses is to be developed. This requires great care upon the part of teachers in selecting and arranging the objects to be used. It also requires equal care in the method of conducting exercises for this purpose. *Second*, a correct knowledge of the nature and properties of material things and clear and accurate definitions are to be secured. This is the result of systematic study and instruction. Ob-

jects used in a rambling way in what is known as object lessons, or for illustrative purposes, fail of this end.
Such a use may, perhaps, be legitimate for other purposes, but not for this.   *Third*, the proper development
of the power of Ideation is at first to be accomplished
almost exclusively in this way.   This is perhaps the most
important thing that can be done for pupils, particularly
during the earlier stages of their work.   Their success
in prosecuting the more abstract subjects of study
depends very largely upon their ability to form correct
and vivid mental representations, not only of objects
of sense but also of every mental object of thought.
The latter, however, is based upon the former, hence
the importance of emphasizing strongly the exercise
of Ideation in connection with the use of objects.

*63.   The mind can exercise only a definite amount of
energy at any one time.   This amount varies with age,
natural ability, and degree of development.*

(*a*). As a necessary consequence of this limitation of
the exercise of mental power, it is evident that the un-
developed mind, such as that of the child, can give
attention only to one thing at a time.   Hence teachers
in assigning work, and in conditioning pupils properly
for its performance, must have careful regard to the
average minimum of mental power their pupils can
exercise.

(*b*). Teachers, in all explanations, in conformity with
this principle, should present only one step at a time,
and each step should be held before the mind of the

pupils until it is so clearly defined that it requires but little energy to hold it while a new step is undertaken. When teachers fail to pursue this course, explanations which may be clear and full make usually only a confused impression upon the minds of the average pupils. Their mental power is not equal to holding before them a clear and vivid representation of a series of steps which have been rapidly presented by the teacher. Hence, they become confused and even discouraged, and, consequently, their own time as well as their teacher's must be wasted in several repetitions of an explanation which, if properly presented at first, would have been understood.

(*c*). In keeping also with this principle, all illustrations used should be simple and familiar, in order not to overtax the energy of the pupils, nor divert their attention and mental strength from the very thing illustrated.

64. *The mind proceeds ¹from the simple to the complex, ²from the known to the unknown, ³from the particular to the general.*

This fixed order of the exercise of mental activity makes it imperative upon teachers to arrange all material made a subject of study by their pupils substantially as follows :

(*a*). So that what is complex or dependent upon other matter is preceded by the elements of which it is composed and the matter on which it depends ;

(*b*). So that the known may stand in such relations

to the unknown as will serve to place the pupils in a position, which will require them to include in their observation of the known the elements of the unknown, by which a correct knowledge of it will be acquired;

(*c*). So that in every case a sufficient number of particulars must be examined before general propositions or statements are formulated.

65. *The mind perceives wholes first, then parts; differences, then similarities.*

(*a*). It follows from this principle that all complex objects of study are perceived, in the first place, in a vague and indefinite manner ; that they are made distinct, definite and comprehensive just to the extent they are [Art. 58 (*d*) to (*g*)] analyzed, by the process of Observation and Comparison, into elements or parts that can be readily and clearly perceived, and to the extent that these elements or parts are again formed into mental units, by an act of constructive Ideation, which correctly represent the objects studied.

(*b*). Wholes that are made objects of study must be such as can be perceived vaguely in a single act of the mind.   When this cannot be done there is no basis presented for mental activity, and hence such wholes cannot in any proper sense become real objects of study.   Here it must be noted that the wholes or units that can be taken in by a single act of mind varies in breadth or size according to the mental power acquired.   Hence it is imperative upon teachers to analyze each object or subject assigned to pupils into such dependent parts or units as are adapted to their average mental strength, and to place before their pupils, as an object of study, only one of these parts at a time.

(*c*). The wholes or units of study assigned to pupils should, in every case, be made clear and comprehensible to their minds by a definite exercise of their own self-activity.   To accomplish this, they must of themselves analyze and form into vivid mental representations the wholes assigned in the manner pointed out in note (*a*).   In this self-effort, if the wholes assigned are properly adapted to the pupils, only such aid should be given by the teachers as will guide their work in a manner to prevent waste of time and energy in wrong directions.

(*d*). Differences attract attention before similarities; hence study, rightly conducted, is chiefly a process of differentiation.   The first step in this process is to distinguish the known from the unknown; then, second, to note the special marks or differences which separate the units or elements of the known from each other.   When pupils have performed these two steps, and can clearly discriminate what they know from what they do not know, and the units or elements of the known from each other, they have laid the right foundation for a successful effort in investigating and mastering the unknown.

66. *The mind can be properly developed and equipped for work only as its experiences are the direct products*

of its own efforts, and as these experiences are by its own efforts transformed into systematized knowledge.

(*a*). It must here be observed that full compliance with this principle does not require that pupils pursue the same course in performing their work as original discoverers. Pupils are, as already stated, investigators and not original discoverers of the principles, laws, attributes, etc., of existing entities and phenomena. Their object is not to discover, but to acquire a correct knowledge of what is already well known and largely formulated, and, in the act of doing this, to develop and equip their minds for future work. To accomplish these three ends in the most effective manner, pupils, in the sense of making their own observations and performing their own experiments, must pursue the course of original investigators. But in no case should they be allowed to waste time and energy in making observations and experiments in the uncertain regions that must largely and necessarily occupy the time and energy of original discoverers. It is the imperative duty of teachers to guard against such a course. They must direct the self-effort of their pupils in such a manner as to exclude entirely that injurious and wasteful line of work, which is of the nature of " Looking for a pin in a haystack."

(*b*). Keeping in mind the facts which have just been stated in note (*a*), the application of this Principle requires that teaching proper, should consist chiefly, if not entirely, of supplying the following :

(1). Conditions or occasions which will enable pupils

to acquire by their own efforts such experiences and knowledge of all objective entities or realities with which they have to do, as these entities or realities should afford them, at the time they are investigated. It should here be observed that the experiences and knowledge which entities and realities are capable of affording are not to be exhaustively acquired at any one time. The extent of the acquisition that should be made at any one time depends upon the stage of development reached by the pupils. Hence care must be exercised by teachers not to attempt to force their pupils to acquire experiences and knowledge which lie beyond the natural limits of their development.

(2). Conditions or occasions which will enable pupils to discover for themselves so much of the truth, and of the principles and laws underlying each subject studied, as will make clear and real all of the elements of which each subject is composed. It will here be noted that it is the effort to discover a given property, principle or law that gives interest, clearness and reality to the knowledge acquired. Hence the importance of insisting that pupils should perform so much of this kind of work as is necessary to secure these ends.

(3). Conditions or occasions which will cause pupils to continue thinking and reasoning persistently upon what is partially or imperfectly known to them until it becomes clearly defined in their minds. Truths, principles, laws, etc., apprehended imperfectly, or in a confused manner, constitute one of the greatest hindrances to the successful progress of pupils in their work.   Hence time is lost and wasted in allowing pupils to pass to advanced work before they thoroughly comprehend the elementary principles on which the advanced work depends.   It must here be noted, however, that this thorough mastery of elementary principles, before passing to advanced work, does not mean that kind of thoroughness which consists in mastering exhaustively useless details.

(4). Conditions or occasions which will enable and cause pupils to arrange and perform their work in such order as will place them in possession, when their work is completed, of a systematic knowledge of the subject studied.   This will require a very careful supervision, by teachers, of every step of the work of the pupils.   It means system in the performance of every step.   But it means especially that pupils should be required, at regular intervals, by careful reflection, independent of all helps from books, teachers, or other sources, to form the details of what they have studied into a system or unit which they are to hold clearly and vividly in their minds as a permanent possession while they proceed with advanced work.

(5). Conditions or occasions which will enable and cause the pupils to express in good form and in their own language, at every stage of their progress, the knowledge they acquire.   The importance of this phase of the pupils' work cannot be over estimated. In the first place, no mental process can be properly completed until its products can be correctly expressed in oral and written form.   But, in the second place, no other acquirements which pupils make are in such constant use or serve such important ends in their life work. An exact use of language is an important help in all mental efforts in which they engage.

67. *The mind reproduces or recalls its former states and experiences through the association of these states and experiences with what is present at the time they are to be recalled.*

(*a*). The proper recognition of this principle in imparting instruction is of first importance. Teachers may be successful in conditioning their pupils so that they can readily gain a correct and clear knowledge of the subjects studied, and yet, at the same time, fail in conditioning them so that the knowledge acquired is made a permanent possession, that can be recalled into consciousness whenever required. This failure results from neglecting to supply conditions, in the act of gaining the knowledge, that will necessitate the formation of sufficiently strong and varied associations to serve this purpose. These associations consist of one or more of the following, which are generally known as laws of memory :

(1). The association of co-existence in time or being immediately successive in time.

(2). The association of co-existence in space or being immediately joined in space.

(3). The association of dependence upon each other, as cause and effect, as means and end, as whole and part.

(4). The association of contrast or similarity.

(5). The association of the sign to the thing signified.

The following suggestions will serve to indicate the way in which the work of pupils should be conducted in order that these laws of association may keep constantly fresh and vivid in their minds the experiences and knowledge acquired:

(*b*). The pupil's work should be conducted in such a manner as will associate, as far as possible, the knowledge acquired with what will occur in the ordinary experience of an average life.

(*c*). The knowledge of facts, principles, laws and processes should always be acquired by the pupils through, and in connection with, the conditions that will actually exist when such knowledge is to be recalled for use in after life.

(*d*). All of the knowledge and experiences of pupils should, in the act of acquiring them, be closely associated with the words that will constitute the working vocabulary of the pupils, so that they may be constantly recalled by the use of these words in practical life.

(*e*). In acquiring a knowledge of a language its words should, as far as possible, be closely associated with the experiences that will occur in the daily life of the pupils and with the words of their mother tongue, so that the vocabulary of the acquired language may, by the ordinary occurrences of daily life, be kept constantly fresh in the mind.

MEANS TO BE USED IN TEACHING.

The nature of the work to be performed by teachers has already been fully outlined   It only remains under the present head to outline the means that should be used in performing this work.   These may be grouped under four heads; namely, the use of special arrangements of work, the use of illustrations, the use of questions, and the use of special directions.

68. *Teachers should condition their pupils for success-ful work by effective arrangements of the matter under investigation and of methods of work.*

(*a*). The work of the pupils should be arranged as a whole, and each daily exercise with the strictest regard to their age, mental development and pecular environments.

(*b*). the arrangement of matter and methods of work should, in every case, be such that each step, when performed, will prepare the pupils thoroughly to undertake the step immediately following with the least possible aid from the teacher.

(*c*). the arrangement of matter and methods of work should also be such that, in the act of performing each step, the inquisitiveness of the pupils will be thoroughly roused with reference to what is still in advance ; in short, should be such as will leave the mind dissatisfied with its present knowledge of the subject under consideration, and will, therefore, create a thirst for farther light and clearer and more extended experiences.

(*d*). The arrangement of matter and methods of work should be such as will naturally and necessarily prepare the pupil's mind to receive and understand all subjects in advance which are directly related to or dependent upon the one under consideration.

(*e*). The arrangement of matter and methods of work should be based upon the laws of association given in Art. 67 (*a*), so that no waste of mental energy will be required of the pupils in fixing the products of their own efforts in the memory in such a way as to be readily recalled into consciousness in their integrity when required.

69. *Teachers should condition their pupils for successful work by the use of illustrations which will place them in a position to understand fully and readily the subject under consideration.*

(*a*). The object of every illustration should be to place the matter under consideration in such relation to the minds of the pupils that they may be able by their own effort to perform the work assigned to them. When illustrations are carried beyond this point they are an injury to the pupils.

(*b*). All illustrations should be selected from what is known and familiar to the pupils; they should be simple and clear; they should be new, striking and forcible, and they should be presented so as to direct attention sharply to the thing illustrated.

(*c*). Illustrations fail entirely of serving the purposes for which they should be used when they are of such a nature, and are presented in such a way, as to fix the attention of the pupils upon the illustrations themselves rather than upon the points to be made plain and memorable by their use. This, however, is the common result when complex and dazzling illustrations are used, as is frequently done in popular lectures upon some of the natural sciences.

70. *Teachers should condition their pupils for successful work by the use of pertinent and properly arranged questions.*

(*a*). This is perhaps the most important means by which teachers can effectively condition their pupils for successful work. Questions should be used to accomplish three distinct ends: namely, to *Stimulate* or generate such mental activity as will fit the pupils to enter with pleasure and earnestness upon the work to be performed; to *Develop* or place the minds of the pupils in effective working relations to what they have to do and to guide them in rightly doing it; to *Test* or ascertain if subjects which the pupils have considered are clearly understood and made a permanent possession. In accomplishing successfully these ends the questions used and the method of using them should be somewhat different in each case. Stimulating questions, for example, need not necessarily be directed to the subject in hand. The object to be gained by such questions is to produce that mental excitation without which the minds of the pupils cannot be put in effective working relations to the matter to be considered. On the other hand, development questions must invariably have their origin in the subject under consideration and, also, must have direct reference to the present efforts of the pupils. But, again, testing questions should take a broader range than development questions. They are intended not only to test how well the pupils have mastered the subject in hand, but also how well they retain the products of their previous efforts and utilize them in the work in their present effort. The following brief ·propositions present, in a general way, the nature, origin, purpose and order of questions to be used as means in the art of teaching.

(1). Questions should be asked in such a manner and should be of such a nature as to stimulate the pupils to question themselves, and to put forth such efforts as may be necessary to master the subjects under consideration without assistance from outside sources.

(2). Each question asked should originate in a present and conscious weakness or difficulty of the·pupil which is clearly perceived by the teacher.

(3). Each question asked should be so expressed and so directed to the pupil's weakness or difficulty as to render the help absolutely necessary in view of the pupil's present condition.

(4). Each question asked should be short and free from ambiguity.

(5). The order which should be pursued in asking questions should always be determined by the condition of the pupil's mind with reference to the result to be secured.

(*b*). It should here be carefully noted that the questions that are to be used, as a means of properly conditioning pupils for their work, are not all to be asked by the teachers. The pupils should be questioners quite as much as the teachers. Indeed, until pupils can ask intelligent questions upon the subjects under consideration, they give no clear evidence that they properly understand these subjects. But more, until they can question themselves closely upon every subject of study, they have not acquired the true power or art of studying. Hence it follows that teachers should encourage their pupils, in every way possible, to form the habit of sharp self-questioning, as a means of solving and explaining difficulties and of gaining clear views of subjects studied.

71. *Teachers should condition their pupils for successful work by giving them such specific directions or suggestions as will protect from waste of time and energy in wrong directions.*

(*a*). The proper use of this means in the teacher's work is very important. It is difficult, however, to determine always just when it is right and best to give specific directions to pupils in the act of teaching. Yet the course indicated by the often-repeated motto, "Never tell pupils what they can find out for themselves," is, to say the least, very unwise. When this course is pursued rigorously great injustice is done to pupils. In many cases it results in complete discouragement and entire neglect of self-effort in performing the work assigned. Difficulties which should be solved, because of their importance in advanced work, are passed over untouched. Pupils in such circum·stances content themselves with doing what is on the surface and can be performed with the least possible degree of self-effort.

(*b*). In the matter of giving specific directions or suggestions, the true motto should be : *Tell pupils just what will save them from a wasteful application of time and energy in finding out for themselves what has little if any value in promoting true self-development and self-equipment.* In practically applying this motto great care must be taken not to tell what pupils should find out for themselves. The following propositions indicate the lines in which telling is admissable :

(1). Specific directions or suggestions should be given to pupils only for the purpose of placing them in a proper attitude or condition to perform the work required by the exercise of their own power.

(2). Such directions or suggestions should never be in the form of specific *rules* which the pupils are required to follow *blindly* in performing their work.

(3). Such directions or suggestions should simply point out to the pupils *just where* and *just how* they can, by self-effort, find the objects of their search or master the difficulties which they encounter.

(4). Such directions or suggestions should always be such as will confine the pupils strictly to the line of self-effort which will best secure the definite results and the general ends for which they are working.

(*c*). Here it should be noted that in many, perhaps exceptional cases, pupils should be placed in possession, in the most direct manner, of information which it is quite possible for them to gain without any help from any source, but in doing so they would waste much valuable time without receiving any corresponding benefit. Of this sort is information, in the study of languages, in regard to special forms of words and constructions which are only of very rare occurrence; of this sort also is information in regard to exceptional devices and contrivances by which alone certain results can be successfully reached in the study of Mathematics, Natural Sciences, etc. In all cases of this kind information should be given to pupils at once. Not to do so is a great mistake.

72. *Only such teachers as possess substantially the following qualifications can use successfully the foregoing means in their classroom work:*

(*a*). Teachers, to do effective work in the classroom, must possess a correct and, in a certain sense, exhaustive knowledge of the subjects on which they give instruction, and also of subjects on which these are dependent. They must also possess a correct knowledge of the present attainments of their pupils, their present and past environments, and of the connection which the subjects under consideration sustain to the knowledge previously acquired.

(*b*). Teachers, to do effective work, must make special preparation on each subject before attempting to present it in class.   They must note with great care the *root thoughts* in each lesson around which details are naturally grouped; they must analyze the subject to be presented into separate, dependent parts or units adapted to the pupils in class; they must prepare pertinent illustrations by which each step in the lesson can be presented properly to the class, and they must fix in their own minds, definitely and clearly, the results they propose, in class, to fix in the minds of their pupils.

(*c*). Teachers should possess the power of holding vividly in their minds, while in the act of conducting their classes, the results which they seek to secure, and the general course the pupils must pursue in reaching these results.   This power is largely the product of constant practice in making analyses and in forming descriptions, definitions, etc., not by recalling the words of another, but from the pictures held in consciousness of the things analyzed, described or defined.   When this course is persistently followed it will develop, in time, the power of forming vivid mind-pictures of everything undertaken.

(*d*). The teacher should possess the power of inventing simple and pertinent illustrations, at the time they are required in class, which will call into service the present knowledge of the pupils, and hence place them in a position to understand the difficulties encountered and to perform the required work.   The exercise of this power depends upon the ability of teachers to perceive quickly and clearly, while performing their work, the difficulties in the minds of the pupils in reference to the results sought to be secured.

THE MANAGEMENT OF SCHOOLS.

The right management of a school constitutes one of the most important conditions which can be supplied for the development of true character. By right management, however, is not meant a mechanical system of rules, false incentives, reports, rewards and punishments, and other devices by which good order may be maintained. These, if they have any place in a rightly-managed school, should be used very sparingly and with much caution. Good order is important, and should certainly be maintained, but it should never be regarded as the chief end to be secured in school management. The following brief outline indicates the leading principles which should guide teachers in this important department of their work.

73. *The management of every school should be conducted in such a manner as to constitute a definite and thorough course of instruction and practice in self-government.*

(*a*). No acquirement which pupils make is more valuable in after life than the power of self-government. This is very pointedly indicated in Prov. xvi., 32 : " He that is slow to anger is better than the mighty ; and he that ruleth his spirit than he that taketh a city "; and also in Prov. xxv., 28 : " He that hath no rule over his own spirit is like a city that is broken down and without walls." The importance of making the management of schools effective instruments in the development of self-government cannot therefore be over-estimated.

(*b*). Intellectual power and right intellectual habits are best acquired in the act of pursuing a prescribed course of study. This is universally conceded; hence the care with which courses of study are arranged for this purpose. Moral power and right moral habits are acquired precisely in the same way. Instruction, for example, in the principles of geometry, in the absence of actual practice in demonstrating these principles, would fail utterly in developing mental power; in like manner, instructions given to pupils in the principles of self-government are of no avail unless the right opportunity is given for the practice of these principles. Hence the management of every school should be so conducted as to give to the pupils this practice.

(*c*). To accomplish in a proper manner the end just stated in (*b*) means that the pupils shall be assigned work in self-government just as regularly and definitely as in arithmetic, grammar, geography, algebra, etc. It means, also, that the work assigned for this purpose shall be rightly adapted to the needs of the pupils, as already fully explained in Art. 56. Infants in years, or in moral development, must not be asked to perform the work which requires the power and judgment of mature manhood. But, while this is true, it is equally true that each must be assigned this kind of work, as only in the act of governing self can the power of self-government be acquired. It is in the act of using the reason, the conscience and the will in directing the conduct of self and of others that these faculties are rightly developed and are placed in full control of the entire being.

74. *The teachers and pupils should be co-partners in the management of schools, and their relation to each other in this work should be controlled by the following general principles :*

(*a*). The *Golden Rule*, " As ye would that men should do to you, do ye also to them likewise," should be the standard by which to judge the right or the wrong of every action.

(*b*). The highest good of the individual, so far as this is compatible with the highest good of the whole school, should be a fundamental principle in determining what courses of action can be legitimately allowed upon the part of teachers or pupils.

(*c*). No requirement should be made of any pupil which would not be right, under similar circumstances, to make of every pupil in the school.

(*d*). The spirit in which everything is done should always be considered more important than the form, and hence should be regarded, both by teachers and pupils, in forming a judgment of the character and value of every act.

(*e*). From the very nature of the relation between teachers and pupils, the teachers must always be considered the proper judges of what is to be viewed, under any given circumstances, as right or wrong. The judgment of the pupils must, however, be carefully consulted, and, before making a final decision in any given case, all the circumstances in any way affecting the case must be fully canvassed.

(*f*). The relations of teachers and pupils are such as to involve a pledge, on the part of both, to regard the interest of each other as sacred, which pledge should always be assumed as given when pupils enter a school.

75. *The course of training in self-government should include such privileges, restrictions and requirements as will give the reason, the conscience, and the will the exercise necessary for their proper development.*

(*a*). The privileges, restrictions and requirements used in school management should invariably be assigned to the pupils as a part of the course of instruction and practice through which they must pass in accomplishing their own self-development and self-equipment. The pupils should, therefore, be led to regard these lines of effort in the same light as their work in literary and other subjects. Privileges, restrictions and requirements should in no case be presented to the pupils in the form of a body of rules, which they must rigidly obey, or else forfeit the confidence of their teachers, and perhaps subject themselves to some form of punishment. Such a treatment of pupils is entirely wrong, and necessarily inflicts upon them permanent injury.

(*b*). Privileges are an important element in developing the power of self-government. They constitute one of the best tests that can be used to determine the trustworthiness of pupils. They must, however, be judiciously granted and carefully graded, according to the ability of pupils to use them rightly. They should also be gradually extended just as the moral strength of the pupils will warrant. In doing this, however, the privileges granted must be such as are strictly in accordance with acknowledged principles of right, and such as can be given to every pupil under similar circumstances; and such also as will promote in the best manner the objects for which the pupils are in school.

(*c*). Restrictions of a certain kind are a necessity in school management, aside from their special use in promoting self-government. They should all, however, be made to contribute, as far as possible, to this latter purpose. This can only be done to the extent they become voluntary. Involuntary restrictions may answer, in an imperfect way, the end of maintaining order, but they fail entirely in developing the power of self-government. Indeed, they have the opposite effect. Pupils who are always kept orderly by the force of conditions which they are unable to resist must gradually lose the power of self-control, and become even untrustworthy when the restraints by which they are held are removed. Hence it is the imperative duty of teachers to avoid imposing restrictions which well-disposed pupils cannot voluntarily accept as necessary to promote the best interests of the school as a whole.

(*d*). Judicious teachers, possessed of tact, can readily get their pupils voluntarily to impose upon themselves just as severe restrictions as may be necessary to maintain the best of order, and, at the same time, test and develop successfully the power of self-contol. Severe restrictions are very important for this latter purpose. Self-control of the highest order can be acquired only under severe conditions. But these conditions, to be effective in promoting this end, must be self-imposed. They must also be reached by a gradual process of development. At first, restrictions imposed should be such as will require no strained effort upon the part of the pupils to comply with them. They should, however, be made gradually more difficult, just as rapidly as the pupils gain the necessary strength.

(*e*). Special practice should be given in this line. Gymnastic and military drill serve a good purpose in acquiring one kind of self-control. But such exercises have little value in developing that self-control which directs the inner workings of the mind, which, for example, puts under perfect subjection the unruly tendencies of the passions. For this purpose a higher order of exercises than gymnastics or military drill must be provided. Pupils must gain this kind of self-control by voluntarily submitting themselves to proper, but severe, restrictions in special lines of conduct. The restrictions imposed for this purpose should, in every case, be such as are in perfect harmony with the principles of right; such as the pupils can readily see will assist them in acquiring the power of self control; such also as necessarily grow out of a sympathetic relation between the pupils and their teachers, and such as will do no violence to any phase of the inherent and natural rights of the pupils.

(*f*). Restrictions are chiefly negative in their nature, and hence train the pupils specially in the exercise of self-denial. They have, however, a positive side also. Not to do, under certain circumstances, is to gain the ability to do the opposite of what may be very agreeable and even strongly pressed upon us. This kind of training is important. Yet it is one-sided and defective unless supplemented by a wide range of positive requirements. These should include not only the duties which pupils owe to themselves, but also the duties and obligations which they owe to others. Selfishness is a deeply-rooted principle of human nature. The exercise, therefore, of self-control under the influence of this principle may be an easy matter, while very difficult when selfishness must be set aside in the interests of others. Hence special attention should be given in the management of schools to making requirements of pupils that will develop in them such a power of self-control and sympathy for others as will fit them to discharge effectively the duties and responsibilities that will come to them in connection with the trying relations and experiences of an active life.

THE TRAINING OF TEACHERS.

The work of teachers, as already pointed out, includes whatever is necessary to be done to develop and equip every phase of the nature of their pupils. Hence the training of teachers, if properly accomplished, must cover each of the qualifications required for the right discharge of the duties and responsibilities which the nature and extent of this work impose. The following brief outline calls attention to the course of instruction and practice by which these qualifications can, ordinarily, be best acquired:

NATURE OF TRAINING WORK.

76. Teaching is, in a marked sense, an art as well as a science. This fact must be fully recognized in every well-directed effort to train teachers for their work.

(a). All training must be based upon the assumption of the possession of a minimum of natural ability; but, whatever the natural ability possessed may be, persistent practice, under the guidance of competent instructors, is the only sure course to attain, with the least expenditure of time and effort, the full mastery of self, and of the principles and processes of the special work for which the teacher is preparing. Artisans and artists alike recognize the truth of this position, hence the practical courses of training to which they submit themselves. The training of teachers rightly conducted must follow in

the same line. The teacher acquires the ability to do successful work, just as the artisan or artist does, by persistent practice under favorable conditions.

(b). The intelligent and practical study of the science of education should be based upon at least a limited experience in the art of teaching. To know aright we must do. "If any man will do his will, he shall know of the doctrine." This principle is now universally recognized as of first importance in the study of the natural sciences. It is, however, doubly important in the study of those sciences in which the *art* or *power to do* is the outcome sought in the examination of every principle. Professional instruction, therefore, in the principles and practices of good teaching can be given in a rational and effective manner, only as it is based upon some previous experience, and is carried on hand in hand with actual practice in the class-room.

77. The instruction and practice given in a properly arranged teachers' training course should cover substantially every line of work for which the student is preparing.

(a). It is not necessary that instruction and practice should be given in every possible subject students may have to teach after they have completed their training course. There are general principles and practices which, when thoroughly mastered, can be applied equally well to the teaching of an entire group of allied subjects, as, for example, languages or the natural sciences. While this is true, it must, however, be carefully noted, that the instruction and practice given in

each group of subjects must provide fully for the modifications of these general principles, which the teachers under training will have to make to adapt their instruction to the actual condition of their future pupils. These pupils will vary in age, environments, capacity, natural and acquired receptivity and energy, and habits of application to mental work. These variations must, therefore, be taken fully into account in the work done in the training course. The training that may fit a teacher to do excellent work in the higher mathematics may fail entirely to give the right preparation for doing good work in intermediate and primary classes. Hence the teachers under training must be graded and receive instruction and practice in the lines which they themselves must follow in grading the pupils they are preparing to teach.

(b). Ability to teach, as commonly understood, is only one, and perhaps not the most important, qualification of good teachers. This qualification fits them chiefly to impart knowledge to their pupils in a natural and effective manner. This is important and well, but the most important function of true teachers is to impart character, true manhood, true womanhood, to their pupils. Where this is not done, the knowledge imparted may prove a snare and a curse to its recipients; hence, in the training of teachers, chief stress should be placed upon supplying conditions that will develop the moral and spiritual sides of their natures, and will also give them the power to produce in their own pupils the same results.

(c). The moral and spiritual training of teachers must be conducted substantially in the same manner as already indicated for other parts of the training work. The discussion of principles of right living, home life, school government, etc., must be conducted hand in hand with actual practice. This will require that the students under training should be made responsible for every detail of the management of the practice school. It will also require that they should be placed in the same relations to the classes they teach as they will sustain afterwards to classes in their own schools. In addition to this they must have actual instruction and practice in giving moral and Bible lessons, and be held responsible for conducting themselves before the school as consistently, **in** every respect, as the regular training-school teachers.

78. A properly conducted teachers' training course must provide appliances and conditions that will rightly promote the development and study of self and also the study of the principles and laws which determine the symmetrical development of the infant, the child, the youth and the man.

(a). Self-knowledge and self-control are among the most essential qualifications of a successful teacher and school-manager. Without these, scholarship and other important qualifications will necessarily fail to be effectively utilized. Hence, in the training course, special attention must be given to this phase of the work.

The maxim " Man, know thyself " must be insisted upon. And to this end, each teacher must be conditioned so as to make self-study a necessity.

(b). Self-study may be promoted in various ways. Among these may be named the free discussion in class of typical cases, and the assignment of work to the students which will expose defects and weaknesses, and also bring to light elements of strength and effectiveness. In these class discussions, while carefully avoiding personalities, the typical cases considered and analyzed must place before the members of the class, as in a mirror, such true representations of themselves as cannot fail to be recognized. The work assigned to promote the study of self must be carefully adjusted to the actual condition and needs of each student. Here the object is to confront each student with such conditions as will necessitate such a correct knowledge of self as must be had in order effectively to remove defects and develop right teaching and managing power.

(c). Teaching and managing power is largely dependent upon the ability of the teacher to assume in a true sense the place of the pupil. " Put yourself in his place " is a maxim that must be followed in all successful school work. Hence, in the training course, special stress must be placed upon this phase of work. The students under training must be required to analyze and trace with accuracy their own personal experience in the act of acquiring a knowledge of the various subjects they are preparing to teach, and also

the conditions and experiences through which they have acquired mental power, right habits, and pure and elevated tastes. They must also be required to analyze and trace in the same manner the experiences through which they have passed in every step of their moral and spiritual development, and in the formation of their present character. This process of retrospection and constant self-examination in the act of training teachers cannot be too strongly insisted upon, as it is the chief exercise by which they are qualified to place themselves in sympathetic and helpful working relations to their pupils.

(*d*). "The study of man is man" expresses a truth which must be carefully heeded in the training of teachers. The study of books on psychology and on the science and art of teaching is valuable and suggestive when the student is properly prepared for such study. This study, however, cannot take the place, in the training of teachers, of the study of the living specimens. By the study of books familiarity may be acquired with what others have said on the nature and constitution of man, but this will fail to cultivate in teachers what will serve them best in dealing with their pupils. Instead of being satisfied with fine descriptions of other men's observations, they must acquire the power, the tastes, and the habits which will enable them to make for themselves the very observations on which these descriptions are based. This is the training teachers need. They must study for themselves, under the guidance of experienced leaders, the living specimens—the infant, the child, the youth and the man. These must be studied in their normal state, amid the various changes and conditions through which they pass in the process of development. This is the kind of training that will place teachers in intimate and living relations to their pupils, that will give them the power of perceiving quickly and clearly the real condition of the minds of their pupils, and hence will enable them rightly to adapt both instruction and management to this condition.

TEACHERS' TRAINING COURSE.

The nature and extent of a teachers' training course must depend upon the nature and extent of the work for which the training is to be given. Hence, before outlining a course, it is necessary to recall some of what has already been said on the true nature of *education* and of the teacher's work.

79. *The process of education has been defined in Art. 3 as that by which external conditions or appliances are made by the action of an agent the means of unfolding or developing symmetrically all the legitimate possibilities of a single life.*

(*a*). Accepting this definition as substantially correct, the process of education involves three elements : namely, the pupil or party developed, the conditions or appliances by which the development is effected, and the teacher or agent who directs the process of development. Each of these three elements has been already fully discussed. Here it is only necessary to note that the possibilities in pupils are of four kinds: namely, physical, intellectual, moral and spiritual, and that conditions and appliances for the harmonious development of all these possibilities must be supplied by the teacher. Hence the training imparted must provide for this fourfold work.

(*b*). Here it must also be carefully noted that the symmetrical development of the four classes of possibilities in the pupil's nature is not the result, as is very commonly supposed, of knowledge imparted by the teacher or acquired from any other source. The acquisition of knowledge is but a small element in the development of character or true manhood or true womanhood. A symmetrical character of the highest order is the product of a pure body, inhabited by a rightly developed intellect, accompanied by right habits and pure and elevated tastes, and the whole subordinate to the control of a rightly developed moral and spiritual nature. Such a character, or any approximation to it, is not the product of acquired knowledge. It is a growth which takes place in the presence of surroundings and conditions embodying the very elements of which it is composed. Just as life comes from life, so character comes from character. To supply the surroundings and conditions that will enable pupils to approximate, as nearly as possible, to such a character, is the special work of all true teachers. For this work, therefore, their training course should thoroughly prepare them.

(*c*). The lines of work by which this preparation can be best effected may be classified under the following heads, namely: Physical Training, Academic or Intellectual Training, Moral and Spiritual Training, and Professional Training. Each of these lines of work, in order to afford the right preparation for teaching, must be conducted, step by step, with special and constant reference to this end. The great object to be accomplished in a training course is to discover clearly to the persons under training the processes, conditions and appliances by which the four classes of possibilities of their own nature have been most effectively developed, and to impart to them at the same time the power, habits, tastes and tact necessary rightly to direct, in the use of these processes, conditions and appliances, in the education of others. The following brief statement of each of these lines of work will serve to indicate the course that should be pursued.

PHYSICAL TRAINING.

80. *The body is capable of a development and training which will give to it special and effective power in school work, especially with primary and intermediate pupils.*

(*a*). The physical nature of pupils of these grades is peculiarly active, and this dominates all of their actions. It is very important at this stage rightly to direct this activity so as to assure a healthy growth of the body. All successful efforts, therefore, for the intellectual, moral and spiritual development of such pupils must regard this fact, and be carried on in harmony with it. Hence teachers, whose physical training has not fitted them to sympathize with, participate in, and direct the physical activities of their pupils, must necessarily fail of proper success in the intellectual, moral and spiritual phases of their work. Without the right kind of physical training teachers cannot, by personal contact or otherwise, supply the conditions and stimuli that are necessary to convert the natural physical activity of their pupils into an invaluable help in other lines of development.

(*b*). The special physical training which should be given to teachers must have reference, first, to the symmetrical development of their own bodies, and second, to the multifarious school work in which the body performs so important a part. Teachers must be examples in all things to their pupils. They must never forget the accuracy with which even young pupils note, read and imitate the elements of weakness and power in their personal appearance and conduct. Where teachers are careless and indifferent in these matters, they necessarily foster, strongly, habits of the same kind in their pupils. The pupils will not usually rise higher in these respects than the example placed before them. This remark is true of the entire range of school work and school requirements. Hence teachers, in order to do the highest kind of work in the school-room, must be able to say to their pupils in every case "*come*," and not "*go*." They must appear at all times before their classes as models of propriety and physical activity, rightly directed, and adapted to every line of work in which they engage.

81. *The physical training given to teachers, in order to be of practical value, must be continued until the bodily changes produced become habits or a second nature, and should cover substantially the following ground :*

(*a*). The systematic development of the body as a necessary condition of true mental development and also of effective physical work. This will require vigorous outdoor sports and exercises, which must be entirely free from the efforts and constraints of games conducted for professional ends.

(*b*). The development of such physical activity as will give sprightliness and gracefulness to every movement of the body. For this purpose systematic training must be given in calisthenics and gymnastics.

(*c*). The practical training of the body, which comes from the constant performance of school work in a systematic, spirited and healthful manner, should receive special attention. This is an important phase of physical training. As already pointed out, the action and personal appearance of teachers in performing their work have a powerful influence in shaping the conduct and character of their pupils. An awkward and undecided manner, for example, not unfrequently destroys, almost entirely, the teacher's power to control pupils. In like manner, an awkward way of working at the blackboard may largely destroy the desired effect, upon a class, of a very clear explanation. Hence the importance of such physical training as will give naturalness, freedom and decision to every motion and position of the body in the act of performing any kind of school work.

(*d*). In the physical training course particular emphasis must be placed upon the development of the organs which have special value in educational work. The sensory organs stand first in this respect. The object to be attained in this case is to make *each sense* a reliable instrument for collecting the necessary data for mental work, and for directing the effective use of the other organs of the body. The training here should be systematic and should include the careful exercise of the senses on a wide range of natural and artificial products, such as the pupils will come in contact with in practical life.

The training of the hand comes second in order. A rightly trained hand is one of the most important qualifications for school work a teacher can possess. Without this, there are several lines of school work which must of necessity be very imperfectly performed. This training should include penmanship, free-hand drawing, the handling and practical application of the various kinds of tools used in the mechanic arts, and the handling and practical use of such apparatus as are necessary in giving instruction in the elements of the natural sciences.   The instruction and practice in this case should be given in the lines of work that possess the greatest educational value, and that will, while training the hand, provide the right material and conditions for the training of the senses.

The next in order is the training of the vocal organs. This should partake of the nature of vocal gymnastics, and should only form the basis of voice culture proper. Special stress should be placed upon such exercises as will impart power to teachers in the use of their voice in teaching, and also in the matter of controlling pupils. The misuse of the voice is, with many teachers, a source of great weakness and the cause of much of the trouble they have in managing their pupils.

ACADEMIC OR INTELLECTUAL TRAINING.

82. *The academic training for primary and grammar school teachers should cover in a thorough manner all the subjects of a good English education.*

(*a.*) This part of the work, so far as it relates simply to mental discipline and the acquisition of knowledge, may be done in good high schools and academies.   In such schools, however, the acquisition of knowledge is regarded as of paramount importance, and hence they fail to place sufficient stress upon the development of mental power, and the formation of right habits and tastes for independent intellectual work. They fail also, almost entirely, in causing the students, while pursuing academic studies, to gain a clear insight into the processes and methods by which their teachers have enabled them to gain the mastery of each study pursued.

(*b*). The defects just pointed out, in the way in which academic work is usually done, in the regular classes in high schools and academies, make it necessary, in order to give students preparing to teach the right kind of instruction, to organize and conduct classes in almost every academic subject exclusively for themselves. Where this is not done, high schools and academies largely fail in giving the preparation necessary to pursue successfully the professional part of the training course. Hence it usually becomes necessary to give to students a thorough review, on the more important or representative subjects, before allowing them to enter upon professional work. In this review special prominence must be given to the features of work referred to in (*a*), which failed to receive proper attention in the first study of the subjects.

83. Students preparing to teach must be required, while pursuing for the first time, or reviewing their academic studies, to give special attention to the following work, and report successfully upon the same, in writing, as a condition to entering upon the professional work.

(*a*). The order in which each topic, in each subject studied, was discussed in class by the teacher.

(*b*). The illustrations and devices used by the teacher to enlist the attention of the students and make plain difficult points in the topics discussed.

(*c*). The methods of drill pursued in fixing permanently in the memory the truths presented in class.

(*d*). The mental processes by which the student himself reached, by the aid of teachers, books, and other surroundings, the solution of every difficulty encountered in the subjects studied.

(*e*). The method pursued and tact shown by each teacher in the management or government of classes, and also the course pursued in the general management of the whole school.

(*f*). The keeping of careful memoranda on the foregoing points in form to be submited for the inspection of the teacher of each class when each subject is completed. These memoranda, and the examinations passed upon each subject, should form the basis from which to judge whether students are prepared or not to enter upon the professional training.

MORAL AND SPIRITUAL TRAINING.

84. *The possession of the right kind of moral and spiritual training is the crowning qualification of the true teacher.*

(*a*). This training has specially to do with the inner life, which is the real source of all outward conduct. Here the requirement is: " Keep thy heart with all diligence, for out of it are the issues of life." Until teachers can do this for themselves, with some degree of success, they are not properly prepared to become the keepers and trainers of the hearts of others. The acquisition of this power is, therefore, imperative upon all teachers. Only by the possession of this can they accomplish the highest good of their pupils.

(*b*). A certain minimum of moral training is possible upon the basis of an unregenerate nature. Only the regenerate heart, however, is capable of the training which develops the highest order of manhood or womanhood, and which prepares, at the same time, for the highest order of service as an exemplar, instructor and leader of others. Without the qualification which this training gives, teachers must fail to come into effective touch, in the best sense, with the moral and spiritual possibilities of their pupils. They must, therefore, fail in a large measure in doing the most important work of their calling.

85. *Successful moral and spiritual training are alike the result of a wise union of instruction and practice.*

(*a*). The key to success in this department of training is found in following Christ's statement, John vii. 17: "If man will do His will, he shall know of the doctrine." The value of moral and religious knowledge simply, in the formation of a true character, is greatly overestimated. The possession of such knowledge in a formal way is compatible with a life of wickedness and immorality. "Devils also believe and tremble." James ii. 19. Devils also know, but they remain devils still. Hence, only that kind of moral and religious knowledge which is evolved out of a life, or which after being acquired from without is embodied in a life, can help to produce a true and reliable character. Hence, also, effective moral and spiritual instruction can be imparted only in the act of practising what is taught.

(*b*). The healthy development of the moral and spiritual natures is as really the product of food and exercise as the healthy development of the body. The food in the former case consists of moral and spiritual truth, in the latter of material substances. The exercise in the former case consists of active service for the good of our fellow-creatures and for the glory of God, in the latter of rightly directed physical exercise and employments. In both cases, to secure the best results, the food and exercise must accompany each other, and must be united in right proportions and be administered at the right time and under proper conditions. The Scripture injunction on this subject is: "Grow in grace and in the knowledge of our Lord and Saviour Jesus Christ." 2 Peter iii. 18. The growth in grace or virtues goes hand in hand with the growth in knowledge. Both are inseparably joined together. As illustrating this necessary union between knowledge and practice in the development of a strong moral and spiritual character, Christ represents the man who *heareth* and *doeth* as the wise man who has acquired the power to withstand the severest storms of this life. "Every one, therefore, which heareth these words of mine, and doeth them, shall be likened unto a wise man, which built his house upon the rock; and the rains descended, and the floods came, and the winds blew and beat upon that house;

and it fell not: for it was founded upon the rock." Matt. vii. 24, 25.

86. *The course of moral and spiritual training should provide such instruction and actual practice as will fix permanently in the mind and heart Bible principles of right living.*

(*a*). This must include such exercises as will develop a vigorous and sensitive conscience—a conscience that will command attention and enforce obedience to its decisions under the most trying circumstances. Such results can be secured only by persistent practice in making careful and critical decisions upon questions of right and wrong. The students under training must therefore be required to examine and pronounce judgment as to the right and wrong involved, in the most trivial as well as the most important matters with which as teachers they may have to do. Here it must be noted that a mistake is very commonly made in regard to the province of the conscience. It is, by many, as has already been pointed out, practically restricted in its operations to what is known as the spiritual side of our nature. Conscience, with such, has nothing to do with ordinary affairs of life and the exercise of the functions of the body. This is a great mistake, and leads to fatal results, especially in the training of infants and children. The decisions of the conscience are co-extensive with our existence and the work of our entire being. They alone settle authoritatively *when, where, how,* and *for what purpose* each function of the body and each power of the mind *ought* to be exercised.

(*b*). In harmony with what has just been stated, the training of the conscience must commence with the infant and be continued up to mature life. In the case of the infant, the consciousness of the *ought* and of the *ought not* accompanies every experience he passes through in which he knows that one of two courses can be pursued, one of which will avoid pain and suffering. As he matures in mind and body, the range of this consciousness extends until it includes every activity of his being. If rightly guided in the educational processes that take place during the periods of infancy, childhood and youth, the habit will be firmly fixed of never acting until the conscience has given its decision as to the right or wrong involved in the course of action proposed. Hence the importance upon the part of teachers under training of making a special practical study of this subject. They should be required to discover by careful observation the peculiar moral tendency of each pupil in their classes, and to record the same in good form for examination by their teachers. They should also be required to accompany this record by carefully prepared suggestions on the appliances that should be used, in special cases, to counteract evil tendencies and strengthen what is good, and thus promote, in the best way, courses of conduct that will crystallize into a strong moral character. The reports made in this way by the student teachers should form the basis of discussion in class on the appliances and methods of moral and spiritual training.

87. *A proper supply of the right kind of moral and spiritual food and of moral and spiritual exercises must be provided in order to secure the successful development of a true character.*

(*a.*) It has already been stated that moral and spiritual truth constitute the aliment for moral and spiritual development.   While this is correct, it is not true that such truth can be used indiscriminately to effect this end.   A careful selection must be made, corresponding with the stage of development reached.   The *milk* is for *babes* and the *strong meat* for those of *mature minds.* In nothing, perhaps, do teachers more signally fail than in adapting the truths supplied their pupils to their actual condition and stage of progress.   This remark applies to all kinds of truth, but especially to moral and spiritual truth.   Hence the great necessity for the careful training of teachers in this department of their work.

(*b.*) The Bible is the foundation of all moral and spiritual teaching.   Its simple and yet comprehensive objective representations cover the entire possible range of human experiences.   Every relation of man to man, of man to God, of man to the present condition of things, and of man to the future state, is objectively and exhaustively presented in the Bible.   The storehouse, therefore, from which to draw moral and spiritual food is complete and inexhaustible.   It requires, however, trained minds and trained hearts, possessed of a correct and sympathetic knowledge of the real condition of the souls to be fed, to draw from this storehouse the very food that will meet the wants of these souls in the most effective manner. The training for this work requires the most careful and painstaking study of the Bible. In this study the Bible must not be treated as a mere literary or historical production, but as a perfect record of objective cases, which reveal clearly and infallibly the operative forces and consequences of all human actions, God's treatment of these actions, and His method of restoring lost human beings to filial affection and to Fatherly favor. This study should be conducted indentively, the same as other subjects.

PROFESSIONAL TRAINING.

Under this head will be outlined the course that should be pursued in giving to teachers the special professional training necessary to fit them for effective service in every department of their work. In this outline it is assumed that the professional course is to follow such physical, academic and moral training as has already been outlined in Arts. 77 to 84 inclusive. It is assumed also that the object of this course is to fit teachers thoroughly rightly to condition their pupils (Arts. 60 and 66) to acquire in the best and most direct manner physical and mental power, right habits, pure and elevated tastes, systematized knowledge and a reliable and symmetrical character (Art. 7). The preparation for such a responsible and far-reaching work as this should be broad and thorough, and should be made under such conditions as will secure the very best results. These conditions are substantially as follows:

88. *A thorough course of reading and instruction in the elements of Mental Physiology :*

(*a*). This line of study can be undertaken with profit only after the elements of Physiology and Hygiene have been thoroughly mastered. In the instruction given under this head man must be regarded as an organized unit composed of body and mind (Art. 4). The course should cover a very careful consideration of the following points:

(*b*). The relation between the nervous system and physical and mental activity, including the special study of the functions of the motor and sensory nerves, the classification of these functions and their products, and the formulating of the laws which relate each class of nerves to its products.

(*c*). The special senses, first, considered simply as physical organs, and second, as the instruments by which the mind takes cognisance of the phenomena of the external world. This should include a careful examination into the nature and extent of the functions and of the products of each sense. It should also include an equally careful examination into the nature and extent of the physical and mental conditions and exercises that must be supplied in order rightly to train or educate each sense.

(*d*). The special kinds of nerve activity that affect directly or indirectly the action of the mind in inquiring sensations and sense perceptions, and also in the exercise of the power of ideation, of memory, of attention and of. imagination. This should also include the careful study of the effects of nerve activity upon the passions, emotions and the action of the will.

(*e*). The sports, amusements and other physical exercises which should be considered as necessary conditions of a healthy and vigorous nerve and mental activity. This should include a careful examination of the principles which should determine the nature and extent of such exercise in connection with school work.

89. *A thorough course of reading and instruction in the elements of Psychology, following the instruction in Mental Physiology:*

(*a*). This course should be conducted with special reference to the work of teachers. Much that is of value and of intense interest to the investigator of psychological phenomena should be entirely omitted. The instructions given should be based largely upon the facts and principles discussed in Mental Physiology, and should follow the order of self-development, Art. 56 (*d*), rather than the logical order of the subject. The following points should be very carefully investigated and the results reached formulated and made a permanent possession.

(*b*). The natural order of primary mental activities, namely sensation, sense perception and ideation; the mental process involved in each of these activities; and the conditions by which this process can in each case be intensified and gradually enlarged in the scope of its operations.

(*c*). The mental process involved in forming concepts and judgments, in acts of imagination, in conducting courses of reasoning, and the progressive nature of the conditions and exercises by which the process peculiar to each of these forms of mental activity can be developed and strengthened.

(*d*). The laws of mental and physical association by which past objects of consciousness are recalled into present consciousness, by which, also, induced states, such as habits and tastes, are stimulated and called into present action; and the manner of conducting every department of school work so as to form strong associations which will, whenever required, readily recall into present service past objects of consciousness and past induced states of body and mind.

(*e*). The mental process called studying; the mental activity or state called attention; and the nature of the exercises by which each of these important forms of mental activity can best be strengthened and properly utilized in performing mental work.

(*f*). The conscience, the emotions and the will; the relations they sustain to each other; the place that each should be given in the educational process, and the exercises and conditions by which each can be developed and made effective in the formation of a true character.

90. *Based upon Mental Physiology and Psychology, a course of reading and instruction in school organization and school management covering substantially the following ground :*

(*a*). The best methods of conducting examinations, of grading, of classifying and of making promotions.

(*b*). The general arrangement of the school, the seating, the use of classrooms, division of time, intermissions and change of classes.

(*c*). Physical exercises, their nature and extent, the management of play grounds and of all out-door sports.

(*d*). Management, general principles, methods of dealing with special cases, legitimate rewards and punishments, suspensions and exclusions when justifiable.

(*e*). The relation of teachers to parents or guardians, the rights and obligations of both parties, how far parents should be consulted in special cases of discipline, the limits of the control of teachers over their pupils.

(*f*). Records, reports, standings, nature and extent of the incentives that should be used; private and public exercises, their nature and extent; literary societies, their place, their management and their influence.

(*g*). Duties of Principals, their authority and respon-sibility; the assignment of work to their teachers; special and general duties of subordinate teachers.

91. *Instruction in methods, or the application of right principles of teaching, based upon clearly defined laws of physical and mental development :*

(*a*). The instruction under this head should first be given in the form of practical discussions upon right principles of teaching and their application to special subjects; then in connection with actual teach-ing in the form of practical hints and suggestions, and of friendly yet rigorous criticism.

(*b*). Principles of teaching have already been out-lined in Arts. 59 to 72, inclusive. In the discussion of the application of these principles it will not be neces-sary to consider all the subjects of an extensive currie-ulum. A careful selection can be made that will meet fully all requirements. Two things should, how-ever, always govern in making this selection : first, the subjects selected should cover every stage of the men-tal development of pupils ; second, the nature of the subjects should be such as will illustrate fully the change of method necessary in the pursuit of different lines of study or investigation.

(*c*). The practice-teaching should be made to con-form as far as possible to the conditions with which teachers will have to do when their training course is completed. Pupil-teachers should be put in full charge of each class they instruct. They should be made responsible for the management and teaching of their classes in the same sense as they will be when conducting a school of their own. They should have charge of each class a sufficient time to test properly their ability in managing and in carrying to a successful finish a definite portion of the subject taught. The time necessary for such a result should vary from five to ten weeks, according to the nature of the subjects.

(*d*). The practice-teaching of pupils should be under the most careful supervision of experienced teachers. This supervision should, however, be conducted in such a manner as to avoid a domineering spirit, which, to a great extent, reduces pupil-teachers to machines in performing their work. The object of the supervision should always be to encourage in every way possible originality and self-dependence in the pupil-teachers. The course of training should not destroy personality. It should rather correct defects, and in this way strengthen it. The following suggestions indicate what may be regarded as the proper course to be pursued by supervising or critic teachers in the discharge of their duties:

(1). They should make it their chief aim to correct effectually root-defects, which, when corrected, will remedy a large number of minor defects. It is a great mistake to indulge in criticising in detail these minor defects. They will, without fail, disappear when the *root* that *supports* them is cut off.

(2). "One thing at a time" is a necessary maxim in

the work of critic teachers, as well as in the work of pupils. Hence the removal of one *root-difficulty* at a time should be a guiding principle with critic teachers. The opposite course is extremely injurious. To spread out in a vivid manner before young and inexperienced teachers all of their weaknesses and defects at one time is not only discouraging to them, but takes from them largely the power of making the corrections in their work that are most important.

(3). Critic teachers should, without fail, commend, upon all suitable occasions, points of excellency in the work of pupil-teachers. This phase of work is frequently partially, if not altogether, neglected. When pupil teachers are properly encouraged by having their excellencies pointed out, they will bear, and indeed solicit, the severe use of the critical knife in cutting off their defects.

(4). The method of getting a correct estimate of the defects and excellencies of the work of pupil-teachers should be varied, according to the peculiar nature and needs of each teacher. The critic who takes a seat in the back or some other part of the room, with note-book and pencil in hand to jot down all noticeable defects, is ordinarily, in the case of young and inexperienced teachers, a very productive *cause* of defects. Such an extreme course as this should be carefully avoided. Critics should visit pupil-teachers in their work in a way that will encourage and inspire confidence, and hence allow them, when the critics are present, to be self-possessed, natural, and able to do at least average work. Critics possessed of proper qualifications can readily gain the confidence of the pupil-teachers, and hence perform their work in this manner.

(5). Hints, suggestions and corrections which are strictly personal should be given to the pupil-teachers privately, and not in the presence of any of their classmates. There are, however, hints, suggestions amd corrections that should be presented in class. In this case all personalities should be avoided. The chief object of this exercise should be to point out the application of right principles of teaching in correcting defects which have appeared in the practice work of some of the pupils. The greatest freedom should be allowed to the pupils, in this discussion, in the way of asking and answering questions, and also in making suggestions and pointing out excellencies and defects in certain methods of teaching and managing.